NEIL GUNN'S COUNTRY

NEIL GUNN'S COUNTRY

ESSAYS IN CELEBRATION OF
NEIL GUNN

Edited by
Dairmid Gunn and Isobel Murray

Chambers

Published 1991 by W & R Chambers Ltd,
43–45 Annandale Street, Edinburgh EH7 4AZ

Acknowledgments

The editors and publisher are grateful to the following
for permission to reproduce photographs:
Dairmid Gunn, Malcolm MacEwen,
Glyn Satterley and the National Library of Scotland

The publisher acknowledges
the financial assistance of the Scottish Arts Council
in the publication of this book

British Library Cataloguing in Publication Data

A catalogue record for this book is available from the British Library

ISBN 0–550–22500–5

Cover design by James W. Murray

Typeset by Buccleuch Printers Ltd, Hawick

Printed and bound in Great Britain by
Butler & Tanner Ltd, Frome, Somerset

CONTENTS

CONTRIBUTORS

GEORGE BRUCE, poet, was a BBC producer from 1946 to 1970, whose main responsibility was arts programmes. He produced two films on Neil Gunn. The first, filmed at Kerrow and Dalcraig, was for *Counterpoint*, BBC Scotland's first television arts magazine. The second, *Light in the North*, commissioned by the Scottish Film Council in association with the Scottish Arts Council, was for the occasion of Neil Gunn's eightieth birthday. Bruce's *Collected Poems* (1970) won a Scottish Arts Council award. His most recent collection, *Perspectives 1970–86*, was published in 1987.

DOUGLAS GIFFORD, formerly a lecturer in the Department of English Studies at Strathclyde University, is a reader in the Department of Scottish Studies at the University of Glasgow. He is author of a full-length book on James Hogg, and editor and contributor to numerous books on Scottish literature, including a memorable work on Neil Gunn and Lewis Grassic Gibbon.

DAIRMID GUNN, a nephew of the author, is co-executor of the Neil Gunn Literary Estate. He spent many years as a career officer in the Royal Navy, during which he saw periods of active service in Korea, Port Said and Cyprus, and spent over two years in the Diplomatic Service in Moscow. A fluent Russian speaker, he is now chairman of the Scottish branch of a UK organization dedicated to improving cultural and economic relations with the USSR.

FRANCIS RUSSELL HART, a graduate of Harvard and former Professor of English at the University of Massachusetts in Boston, is the author of *The Scottish Novel*, *Scott's Novels* and *Lockart as a Romantic Biographer*. A friend and admirer of Gunn, he is co-author of that writer's biography, *A Highland Life*.

NAOMI MITCHISON, daughter of the physiologist J. S. Haldane and sister of the scientist J. B. S. Haldane, and a great friend of Neil Gunn, was born in Edinburgh in 1897 and educated at the Dragon School, Oxford, and at home. She married the Labour politician G. R. Mitchison (later Baron Mitchison) in 1916. Socialist, feminist and inveterate traveller (she is an official tribal mother to the Bakgatla of Botswana), and from 1947 to 1965 a member of the Highland Panel, Naomi Mitchison is the author of over seventy books – historical novels, science fiction, autobiography, short stories and children's books.

ISOBEL MURRAY is a senior lecturer in English at Aberdeen University. In 1984, with Bob Tait, she published a collection of studies on ten modern Scottish novels and is currently conducting a series of in-depth interviews with Scottish writers. A by-product of these interviews are her two editions of Naomi Mitchison's work. She reviews new Scottish fiction for *The Scotsman*.

J. B. PICK, novelist, poet and critic, lives and writes in Kirkcudbrightshire, Scotland, and is the author of *The Last Valley* and co-author of *The Strange Genius of David Lindsay*. A great friend of Neil Gunn's, he is also co-author of the authoritative biography of Gunn, *A Highland Life*.

INTRODUCTION

NEIL GUNN, one of Scotland's most distinguished twentieth-century authors, wrote his first book in 1926 and his last thirty years later. Although certain themes remained central to Gunn's writing, the author's emphases and interests changed with the passage of time. His life was always a pilgrimage towards truth and understanding. This year is the centenary year of his birth; it also marks the passing of a period of seventeen years since his death. This second fact is important. The number of people who knew him well and were able to discuss his work with him is diminishing. There is some urgency, therefore, in squeezing from the recollections of such people the last drops of knowledge, speculation and appreciation to create the distillate that gives this book its name, *Neil Gunn's Country*. In this context, I cannot but think of that most spiritual and magnificent of the Gospels – the Gospel of St John – an account of Christ's life and teachings written by a witness to them after a gap of almost seventy years. I hope the saint will forgive me when I write that his distillate, remarkable for its clarity and accessibility to both Jew and Gentile, was as clear and pure as a Highland malt whisky. From this comparison between subject and witness, I am not implying that there is any sort of 'discipleship' in the relationship between Neil Gunn and his friends; I am simply stating that seventeen years can give those who knew him so lovingly and well an opportunity of yet again assessing what this particular author meant to them. It is also a chance for a final salute and farewell.

When Richard Drew, now of Chambers, approached me on this subject, my first reaction was to query the value of yet another book on Neil Gunn. Like many of my friends, I was only too aware that my uncle had already been blessed by that most subtle, gentle and perceptive of biographies, *A Highland Life* by John Pick and Francis Hart. Was there anything more that could be written, was the question that I had to answer. How reassuring for me it was when the two biographers accepted the challenge to write one last thing about the man who had meant so much to them as literary genius, companion and friend. Others were not slow to join in and the book took shape.

The book does not pretend to be narrowly scholarly. It is on the one hand a mix of the literary and metaphysical, and, on the other, personal recollections, with insights into the author's personality and character. All the ingredients are important for the understanding of this remarkable writer and for what he stood. There is something here for everyone who is interested in life and its meaning. For those not acquainted with this writer there is sufficient matter in the essays themselves to titillate their appetite for some of Gunn's fare.

The title *Neil Gunn's Country* is aptly chosen. There is a *double entendre* in the choice of the title as the country is being looked at on two levels: the actual landscape of the Highlands, and that other landscape where there is a quest for deeper spiritual insights into the whys and wherefores of life on this earth and a more profound understanding of the significance of history in life's rich pageant. In Gunn's work the two landscapes are always there, beckoning the reader to interpret and speculate in an attempt to make some sense of the vagaries of the human situation.

That these most accomplished of biographers, John Pick and Francis Hart, can write something new about Gunn and his work is a tribute to both them and to the author. In his illuminating essay, 'Neil Gunn and the Eternal Landscape', John Pick points out that Gunn uses limited material again and again, but never writes the same book twice. This assertion becomes clearer when Pick writes about Gunn's approaches to the novel. 'There are three types of approach: descriptions of experiences with a visionary, "second sight" quality; a rather self-conscious use of rhetoric to indicate "otherness"; and the daily landscape and events described with such exact insight that they acquire an abnormal clarity.' To illustrate the last approach Pick selects a sentence from *The Shadow*, a book in which Gunn describes the recovery of a young Scottish woman (Nan) returned from London after a nervous breakdown – a recovery in which nature played its part. 'The yellow crocus was a tuning fork out of some sunny underworld, still holding the glow of the note.' On this, Pick comments: 'Nan's sensitivity to natural growth is a sign of her recovery. To feel the world breaking into spring is her way of building sanity and faith . . .'

It comes as no surprise to remember that it was Pick who shared Gunn's interest in Zen Buddhism and maintained a dialogue with him on Eastern thought. This profound understanding on the part of Pick to a different approach to living, shared by Gunn, is covered most appositely when he writes: 'The country of the spirit is the country of the eyes and the mind; it takes shape as the eye sees more and the mind understands more. For Gunn you arrive "elsewhere" when you are most alertly *here*; but for this there is a necessary prerequisite. As it says in *The Well at the World's End*, "All he had to do was to forget himself. Immediately the ego with its demands was forgotten, everything was alive naturally in its own place . . ."' But as Pick wisely points out: '. . . to forget yourself is the most difficult thing in the world to do.'

In his essay 'The Elemental in Neil Gunn', George Bruce, nearer to Neil Gunn in terms of age, vividly recollects the impact made by Gunn's *Morning Tide* on the sophisticated and world-weary readership of the 1930s. Within such a readership, whose diet was intense subjective literature, what place had a novel set in an obscure fishing community in the north of Scotland? Yet the critic F. R. Leavis was bowled over by it, and perhaps this is understandable when such a passage as this is to be found in it. It describes a boy sitting on a deserted beach.

Below the high-tidal sweep of tangleweed the beach sloped in clean grey-blue stones rounded and smooth, some no bigger than his fist, but some larger than his head. As he stepped on them they slithered and rolled with a sea noise. The noise rose up and roared upon the dusk like a wave. All around no life was to be seen, there was no movement but the sea's.

Bruce argues that the elemental was at the heart of the consciousness of Gunn. His principal characters, and especially the young and the old, are drawn in the context of natural forces. There is a biblical simplicity and depth in this, and the dignified cadences of the King James' version of the New Testament can be felt in Gunn's prose. The elemental in Gunn comes over vividly in terms of gender in *Highland River*. 'The abiding calm of his mother, old as the earth; the cleaving force of his father, like the bow of his boat.'

What is implicit in Bruce's essay is that in Gunn's work the measurement of man, woman and child as persons is made in the presence of the elements, to which in *Neil Gunn's Country* there is a right and a wrong relationship. There is much in the vivid and moving end to Bruce's essay: 'At the end of the film *Light in the North*, made in 1972, Neil Gunn is seen against sea and sky. The last word he spoke as commentary was "Miracles".'

If Pick and Bruce concern themselves in this book with the timeless element in Gunn's work, then Douglas Gifford firmly places the work within the context of the Scottish literary tradition. He argues that since the Jacobite rebellions the Lowlands and the Highlands have existed in a state of cultural division. Sir Walter Scott tried to create a new way of looking at the Scottish identity and history in his trilogy of *Waverley*, *Old Mortality* and *The Heart of Midlothian*. In Gifford's view, even Scott failed with his new Scottish myth because his view ultimately saw Scotland submerging its identity in Britain. He sees Gunn in his trilogy of *Sun Circle*, *Butcher's Broom* and *The Silver Darlings*, followed by the epic duality of *Young Art and Old Hector* and *The Green Isle of the Great Deep*, plumbing the depths of self-doubt and historical agony, yet triumphantly emerging with a mythic refashioning of identity and an affirmative statement that the Highlands and Lowland Scotland could turn tragedy into positive recovery. Gifford claims that the later novels prove that this regeneration is the only true match for the destructive materialism, scientific rationalism and political authoritarianism of the twentieth century. In a dramatic assertion of the achievement of Gunn he writes: 'The achievement is Tolstoyan, to my mind amounting to perhaps the greatest and most affirmative and most artistically effective and coherent contribution to Scottish literature and to Neil Gunn's country, on a par with MacDiarmid's *A Drunk Man Looks at the Thistle.*'

Naomi Mitchison also confines her essay on Gunn to within more concrete boundaries, but is content to assess him as a man and friend. She describes her correspondence with him, started in 1941, as something of a 'conversation'. Both were accomplished writers, who delighted in discussing matters of craft and skill, and condemning the occasional obtuseness of publishers; both, in differing degrees and directions, were interested in politics – particularly politics pertaining to Scotland. Mitchison, the more forthcoming and public figure of the two, would chide Gunn for his dislike of the public occasion and for what could be described, albeit misleadingly, as a form of escapism. With regard to her he had his role to play, proffering advice and comfort on matters concerning social relationships. One such letter concerns Mitchison's problems as the lady in the Big House at Carradale:

> Complicated personal relations are the devil at any time, but when social, class etc relations are added, the old Cretan maze has nothing on 'em. Being as you fondly believe . . . a classless human, you may forget . . . how subconscious social elements do their work in eager hearts . . . Come off it a bit and smile. But never give in by an inch.

The war years may have been drab and depressing but there was much to discuss: the failure of totalitarianism, both fascist and communist, and what sort of new world would emerge from the ashes of the conflict. This correspondence probably caused Gunn to embark on possibly his most ambitious novel, *The Green Isle of the Great Deep*. Although Mitchison described her correspondence with Gunn as conversations, they could not be regarded as a substitute for meetings. When they did meet in February 1943, it was a joyous occasion full of fun, laughter and spontaneity. An extract from Mitchison's diary of that time says it all, and in an inimitable way.

Hart came into Gunn's life much later but he quickly established a profound rapport with him. His contribution to this book has as its theme the idea of handing Gunn on to a new readership. Like his co-biographer John Pick, Hart has a deep knowledge of Gunn's work and of Scottish literature in general. He tackles the handing-over process in epistolary form. In a letter to me he discusses the task facing him and the way in which he can induce more interest by suggesting paths for exploration by others. In this search for essentials there is room for many approaches to a life that lasted eighty-one years and a creative output of well over twenty major works.

The second letter is to a mature reader who has encountered a novel of Gunn's for the first time and wants to know more about the author. Hart handles this most delicately and sympathetically, drawing particular attention to that most personal of novels, *The Well at the World's End*, about which he writes: 'Nowhere is Neil more at home with or closer to his central figure . . . Peter [the central character] combines two sides of Neil: the speculative man – Peter is a history professor – and the practical countryman – Peter is son of a famous shepherd.'

His letter to John Pick is special, being as it is the beginning of yet another dialogue between two discerning and cultured men. The letter implies a meeting of minds and represents literary criticism and interpretation at its highest level. In discussing *Highland River* and *The Serpent* Hart moves into the misty realm of Gunn's changing intuition of women. He finds a key in the latter novel when he writes:

> Tom [the central character] is led to this revelation by his reading, by his discovery in Rousseau of 'the feminine mind', as opposed to the 'male categories, the philosophical absolutes, the masculine rules of life'. This is the only place I know of in Neil [Gunn] where he acknowledges that the 'feminine' is not necessarily a matter of gender.

With this idea of the feminine pervading the end of his letter to Pick, it is appropriate that his last letter should be addressed to a woman, a young person who was one of his students in Boston in the 1980s. It is the final handing over of the baton by a man whose modesty and humility in themselves must be an example of the attributes of a true teacher. Recalling *The Silver Darlings*, the book through which he had introduced his students to Gunn, Hart moves on in his letter to *Bloodhunt* and *Young Art and Old Hector*. In Sandy, the central character in *Bloodhunt,* Hart claims that here is a male character who has effectively assumed the traditional role of the woman – 'the housekeeper, the practical caretaker, the instinctive protector against male categories of law and justice'. Sandy is both 'paternal and maternal'.

But Hart ends with drawing his former student's attention to *Young Art and Old Hector.* The importance of secrecy in a positive sense is contrasted with the horror of betrayal, a sin categorized by Gunn as being on a par with cruelty. The letter, like the book itself, shows the wonderful relationship that can exist between the young and the not so young. It is thrilling to see a letter from one American to another on the meaning of the work of a Scottish author. It is a supreme example of the universal appeal of Gunn's work and in this context the quotation that Hart selects from *Young Art and Old Hector* is so appropriate: 'It's not the size of the knowing that matters, I think, it's the kind of the knowing.'

In my own essay on Neil Gunn, 'My Uncle and I', I have anchored my knowledge of him in time and place. The impressions that I have of him were garnered by me in childhood, youth and middle age. I hope these impressions and recollections will add something to the general understanding of Neil Gunn; I also hope that this book will provide directions for those who wish to set out on their own journey of discovery in Neil Gunn's country.

DAIRMID GUNN

MY UNCLE AND I

MY UNCLE AND I

Dairmid Gunn

There was a Door to which I found no Key;
There was a Veil past which I could not see.
Omar Khayyam

NEIL GUNN first came into my consciousness when as a small boy
in 1938 I moved with my parents from Edinburgh to live in the
village of Strathpeffer near Dingwall in Ross and Cromarty. My father
John, one of Neil's two younger brothers, had become HM Inspector
of Schools for the county – an appointment that was to keep him
there until after the war. At the time of our move Neil and his wife,
Daisy, had just rented Braefarm House in the hills to the north of
Dingwall and Neil was settling down to his first year as a full-time
writer.

For a child an uncle can play a very important role in his or her life.
He is almost one of the family, but not quite. There is that element of
distance that can make him a friendly stranger, someone on the outer
circle of family life. In Russia the benevolent stranger is often
addressed by a child as Uncle, a form of address that emphasizes trust
and security on the child's part. For me Neil represented the
archetypal uncle, a person whom I accepted as a friendly force within
my immediate landscape of early childhood. I was also blessed by
having Neil's youngest brother Alick, who lived in Caithness, as the
other uncle with whom I became quickly acquainted. A delightful
person full of humour and fun, and deeply liked and respected in the
county. But he was the holiday uncle, the one strictly associated with
summer holidays in Dunbeath, the village where my paternal
grandfather had lived. Neil was and remained 'the uncle'.

My father and Neil were inseparable friends. The fortuitous accident of their living close to one another during the war years meant the frequent exchange of visits. Often these included my mother, my brother Alasdair and myself. Indeed, the Sunday afternoon tea at Braefarm House soon became an institution. The difference between the village of Strathpeffer and the countryside round Braefarm House was immense. At the turn of the century the village had developed into a famous spa and boasted a railway station for ease of travel for those from afar. Round the pump room, the centre of the village, was a fine selection of solidly built Victorian and Edwardian houses. The inhabitants of the village included many worthy people who had spent most of their lives in the remotest parts of the Empire or down south in the big cities of this country. In short, the atmosphere was more cosmopolitan than Highland. Braefarm House represented another world. This stone-built house, on the high ground to the north of the strath connecting Dingwall to Strathpeffer, faced south, and, from my uncle's study-cum-sitting-room, views could be obtained of Dingwall, the Cromarty Firth and Knockfarrel, the hill across the valley. Behind the house there was a gradual ascent through typical farm- and croftland to the moors and distant hills. For me this represented another world, a world that was to become my Uncle Neil's country.

It was not long before I realized that my uncle was different from the other adults I knew. The bookcase in our drawing-room in Strath-peffer was full of books with his name printed boldly on the dustcovers. Braefarm House itself possessed an atmosphere that impressed me with its sense of warmth and mystery. The book-lined shelves, the pipe-racks, the pictures, the chiming clock, and above all the immensely comfortable easy-chair in which my uncle always sat. For me, as a child, it had the look of a throne, but a throne devoid of any sense of formality or awe. Nevertheless something inside me made me treat it with great respect. After all, it was the chair from which my uncle seemed to conduct the relaxed and friendly conversations of these Sunday afternoons. He was an accomplished conversationalist for he was prepared to listen – even to remarks and observations made by my brother and me. His attitude when talking to us was never condescending, only courteous. Even at that age, we both were acutely aware that we were in the presence of someone who spoke with a gentle authority and completely without arrogance or self-esteem. Wisdom seemed to bubble out of him, just like his infectious laughter. 'Well, it's like this,' was the well-known introductory phrase and then the brilliant analytical mind would come into play.

I cannot leave the subject of atmosphere without dwelling on someone who was of immense importance to me when I was a child, and in later life, my Aunt Daisy. When studying Latin I learnt of the penates and lares, the household gods of a Roman family, the gods of the hearth. Aunt Daisy indeed was the goddess of the hearth, the spirit of the house, and a creative and benevolent one at that. Her presence was always subtly there; her movements were graceful and quiet and there was a stillness about her that was difficult to define. If she was the spirit of the house, she was also the spirit of the garden. As I have used the Roman penates and lares in connection with the house, I shall use Persephone, goddess of vegetation, to describe my aunt's activities in the flower-beds and rockeries. She was part of the garden and everything she touched seemed to grow and bloom. When describing Aunt Phemie in *The Shadow*, my uncle had his wife in mind. There is no better description of her than this: 'She is comfortably slim and though well over forty the gold in her hair has not faded much. I suppose gold doesn't. She is a tirelessly energetic worker and yet can stand quite still.'

These early memories of my uncle and aunt are mingled in my mind with impressions of the war years, when the area round Strathpeffer and Dingwall was used for military training. My uncle enlisted in the intelligence section of the local Home Guard and I have vivid memories of him calling in at our house for a glass of sherry prior to attending a training session at an army intelligence centre. He wore a uniform of a sort, but there were problems, and Daisy had to perform some feats of tailoring to ensure his balmoral fitted. His experiences of military training both interested and amused him. His account of a total defeat in a mock battle at the hands of the free Norwegians still remains with me. Having to face Norwegians, albeit in a friendly way, brought to his mind the Viking incursions, so colourfully described in *Sun Circle*. As I was to find out later, the war years were a period of immense intellectual activity for him. Amidst all the turmoil of a world at war he produced that masterpiece of creative writing, *The Silver Darlings*. Even as a child I was aware that with this novel my uncle had done something special. Everywhere the book was being talked about. I remember seeing copies of it in the hands of those tolerant adults who travelled in the school bus from Strathpeffer to Dingwall. On one occasion, the bus stopped at the end of the farm road leading to Braefarm House to take on passengers. At that precise moment my uncle was standing nearby as if waiting for someone. A lady in front of me said in a loud voice to her companion, 'There's Neil Gunn, the author.' Immediately, all was silent in the bus and heads were turned to the left. There he was, that tall, elegant, loose-limbed man, dressed in a greenish-blue tweed suit and leaning on his walking-stick with a nonchalant and detached air. A battered hat with brims down fore and aft concealed the high forehead and the shock of fine grey hair through which he liked to pass his fingers. That mental snapshot of my uncle was to remain with me after our family had moved again – this time to Lanarkshire.

As a teenager I visited Braefarm House during school holidays. I had begun to read my uncle's work, possibly more from a sense of curiosity than a desire to broaden my horizons. My family was living in Bothwell near Hamilton in Lanarkshire and, like most young boys in the Glasgow area, I had become mad on sport. Football and cricket obsessed me and yet when I walked with my uncle up the slopes of the Heights of Brae, I was conscious of something I had been missing. The moors, the croftlands and the extensive views to the south were one thing; the company of my uncle another. He listened with easy tolerance to my outpourings on my joy in being 'back' to the scenes of my childhood. He mentioned that my favourite team, Hamilton Academical Football Club, had a name that had appealed to the great T. S. Eliot himself. He guided the conversation persuasively and easily in a direction that made me feel that I was truly participating in a dialogue between equals. The walk over, it was back to that warm and easy atmosphere of Braefarm House, a chiming clock, plenty of books and my Aunt Daisy. These visits as an adolescent contributed richly to my growing sense of awareness of the privilege of having access to an uncle and aunt who had something immensely important to offer me. I had begun to realize that it was not just the beautiful Highland landscape that had captivated me but rather its transfiguration by my uncle.

In 1949 I entered the Royal Navy as an executive officer cadet and began my training at Dartmouth. In the same year my uncle and aunt had to leave Braefarm House, where they had been tenants, and seek another house. They bought Kincraig, an attractive house built in very much the same style as Braefarm House, but with a very different situation. Wedged between the Dingwall and Evanton roads, the house had an uninterrupted view of the Cromarty Firth and the Black Isle. My uncle's study was to the seaward side of the house and bore an extraordinary resemblance to the one he had just vacated. Daisy's deft touch gave the impression that the room had simply been transferred from Brae. But there were differences, as I was to find when I visited them during my first summer leave. There was little room for the afternoon walk and my uncle had to content himself with walking back and forth along a narrow path skirting the foreshore of the firth. My description of his exercise periods as walks, quarterdeck style, amused him and prompted many questions from him about my training for a naval career. Clearly the sea fascinated him, but I felt, even then, that he would have been disappointed with certain aspects of modern seafaring. So much emphasis on radar and other navigational aids; less time for an increased awareness of sea and stars. Certainly Kincraig did not provide him with the space for walking so essential to him. He felt hemmed in, and then there was the noise of the passing cars. The noise element was perhaps relative. A visiting Swedish intellectual who sat quietly during an hour's conversation between Neil and a local friend suddenly interrupted the talk by saying, 'I have heard the second car.' This remark amused my uncle but did not turn him from his decision to find another house.

Daisy and he moved to Kerrow, a fine large house on the right bank of the River Glass near Cannich in Inverness-shire. With the house went a stretch of salmon-fishing; it all seemed idyllic and his friends thought that this would be the ideal place for my uncle and aunt. For many reasons, it was not, and the period at Cannich was to see the end of my uncle's output of books. At this time I had finished my naval training and taken part in the war in Korea and in the landings at Port Said. I kept in touch with him by means of the occasional postcard or letter; my parents, of course, frequently mentioned the 'Brae folk' in their letters. While I was spending the long and tedious hours in Port Said after the invasion in 1956, I received from him his last book, *The Atom of Delight*. I was completely transported by this remarkable spiritual autobiography; it was as if I had come across an oasis after a long journey in the desert. It was the most wonderful and appropriate present I could have received and the timing was perfect. It stirred within me an immense desire to read my uncle's work once more. The beginning of the book fascinated me and has haunted me ever since. 'Often when looking for a thing I find something else. I knew what I was looking for, but what I find is surprising.' Suddenly, Port Said harbour seemed far away; I was back in Neil Gunn's country.

Shortly after this I was serving in a destroyer on a commission that embraced a period of service in the North Sea. On going on to the bridge one day I was amazed to see the unmistakable landmark of Dunbeath Castle on the port beam, and then there was that familiar harbour and those formidable grey cliffs. My captain, a Scotsman, and a great admirer of Neil's early books, was to be the recipient of my expressions of delight at seeing the beaches of *Morning Tide* and the estuary of *Highland River*. Without hesitation, he ordered the navigating officer to take the ship into the inner part of the bay. A great moment for me and, I am sure, for him. My father was not slow to relay the news of this brief incursion into the bay to my uncle. Days later I received a cheque from Kerrow for ten pounds, big money in those days, as a reward for my enthusiasm for the place. My uncle was thinking of his father and how pleased he would have been to be told that the Royal Navy had shown a peaceful interest in his stretch of sea. No press-gang here; only a grandson returning to pay his respects.

If that incident had appealed to my uncle for various reasons, other encounters with the navy were not to his taste. During one of his visits to Edinburgh my mother asked him to join a group of my colleagues who were our guests for dinner. One of these, a particularly talkative man from the home counties, clearly did not live up to my uncle's expectations of what the navy stood for. The thoughtfulness, the sparkle and the reticence that disguises quiet confidence were absent and the man was described next morning to my mother as being just like a 'stockbroker'. I do not think that he considered that stockbrokers were any worse than any other grouping of people; he simply felt that this man did not live up to his idea of the mariner. For him, the wonder and magnificence of the sea deserved to be reflected in the character of those who toiled on it. My uncle was disappointed when people could not be moved by the strength and beauty of nature, on land or sea. On one occasion he had travelled with a lawyer through a stretch of landscape in Ross-shire that was breathtaking in its loveliness. His companion's conversation dwelt solely on the question of fishing rights and the opportunities there were for a quick profit. My uncle summed up the experience as a form of betrayal, a betrayal of the senses.

If my uncle expected so much of those who sailed the seas, then he certainly condoned what is known in naval parlance as a good run ashore. For the mariner the run ashore after a long period at sea has a significance that is difficult to explain to the landlubber. The few hours ashore possess an exuberance and an intensity all their own. I always likened my uncle's visits to Edinburgh to this naval experience. When he was in Edinburgh, he was there to enjoy himself. His programme varied from day to day, even from hour to hour. Visits to friends intermingled with short meetings in pubs and he was accorded the great honour by my mother of always being given the key of the door. On one or two occasions I accompanied him on his visits. It was then that I became aware of his pride in his Celtic background and his consciousness of the naturally aristocratic qualities of the Highlander. With my father he had often discussed the conflicting forces at work in the Gunn psyche. My father contended that the Norse strain was stronger in the family; my uncle was of the view that the Celtic influence was predominant. I was content to settle for a draw and leave it to that book about the genesis of Caithness, *Sun Circle*:

> Out of the North come grey shapes and long seas and men, the North which is worn smooth by the austere winds that have searched out all the faults and cleansed them with the dry fine sand that eternity filters through time . . . Before the eye reaches the Orcades once more, it turns for rest into a sea valley, and in a little glade comes upon a young woman playing with a child.

The Norsemen conquer and are conquered.

My uncle and aunt spent their last years together near North Kessock on the Black Isle. The house, Dalcraig, had a pleasant atmosphere and the front rooms looked on to the Beauly Firth. Ill-health marred these years and when Daisy's death came, it was a great blow to my uncle. She had been a wonderful companion throughout his literary career. The inscriptions for her on the books bear ample testimony to a deep and lasting partnership. She, after all, had been the first to handle his manuscripts, transmuting them into the printed word. During a visit I made to Dalcraig shortly after her death, I remember him asking me to read aloud many of the tributes paid to her in the numerous letters of condolence. One particular letter appealed to him greatly. I cannot remember who wrote it or the exact wording of it. It mentioned most beautifully her ability to make things grow and bloom – an ability that was not just confined to the world of plants. Neil's response was immediate. 'That was just right, and very nice,' he murmured, drumming the arm of his familiar chair with the fingers of his right hand.

Although Daisy had gone, her influence remained. Dalcraig did not lose the atmosphere of warmth and intimacy that she had created. It was as if she was always about to appear. My uncle was blessed with having a series of excellent housekeepers, whose loyalty to him could not have been exceeded. They worked for him during the years when my father, also a widower, spent considerable periods of time as a most welcome guest. For him it was home from home, from which he always returned physically and mentally rejuvenated. This close tie between the brothers was also of profound importance to my uncle. The book that was the manifestation of this great friendship was *Highland River*, still my favourite book. The dedication is to my father and it explains much.

Dear John,
This can hardly be the description of our Highland river that you anticipated when, lying on our backs in a green strath, we idly talked the idea over. Certainly it is not the description I anticipated myself. Some ancestral instinct, at first glimpse of the river, must have taken control and set me off on a queerer hunt than we have yet tackled. Or am I now trying to cover up the spoor? You will realize that though there is no individual biography here, every incident may have had its double. Some of the characters seem to have strayed in from *Morning Tide* under different names. I cannot explain this odd behaviour – apart from this old desire to be in on the hunt in any disguise. However, if only I could get you to see the hunt as a poaching expedition to the source of delight we got from a northern river, I feel you might not be altogether disappointed should you come back (as we have so often done in our time) with an empty bag.
With brotherly affection,
Neil

There was certainly no individual biography. My father is the Kenn of the epic fight between boy and salmon, and the young soldier on the Western Front, and there is a distinct resemblance between him and the physicist. It says much for my uncle's ability to listen to others that the book almost appears to be an autobiography written in the third person, anticipating, as it does, his last book, *The Atom of Delight*. This ability to transmute some of my father's experiences into something vivid and personal is also shown in the storm scene in *Morning Tide*, a scene witnessed by my father as a boy of twelve. The seemingly autobiographical touches in both books represent the charting of a life of the mind, both his mind and those of others with whom he was close. Charting implies a journey and my uncle was always on a voyage of discovery. He liked to gauge the reaction of other people to his ideas and in this respect my father always performed a vital function. His responses were ever important to my uncle and, even when the writing years had ended, the philosophical discussions continued. After all, the hunt was still on.

It was during what could be called the barren years that I always allocated time from my periods of leave to spend a few days with my uncle at Dalcraig. Any time with him was in the nature of a retreat, a chunk of time isolated from the daily round, during which I was conscious of an all-enveloping sense of peace. From the moment I was met off the ferry at North Kessock by this tall figure in tweeds and battered hat and conveyed to the house on the hill, I was in another country, Neil Gunn's country. Yet there was nothing awe-inspiring about my host. He quickly welcomed me into his daily routine of walks, rest periods and the ritual of the evening drams. Always one before the meal and sometimes one after. It was during the walks and in the evenings that opportunities for easy and relaxed conversations came. The walks along the Beauly Firth towards Ben Wyvis would bring us into contact with wildlife from both sea and hill. The quiet discussions in the evenings distilled many of the impressions gained during the day. And as I have used the word 'distilled', I cannot but remember the dram – offered by Neil as something special. The pouring of the liquid and the addition of the touch of Highland water possessed a sacramental quality. In *Whisky and Scotland* he writes: 'The essential oils that wind in the glass uncurl their long fingers in lingering benediction and the nobler works of Creation are made manifest.'

To walk with him was a joy, as he was a countryman who understood his environment and who could dwell on the pleasures of a childhood spent in the enchanting surroundings of a remote Highland strath and in the gentler ambience of a Kirkcudbrightshire village. His admiration for Wordsworth had clung to him and he felt that he had shared many experiences with the Lakeland poet. These experiences had formed the bedrock of his creative aspirations. In this respect the following lines from *The Prelude* are most appropriate.

> There are in our existence spots of time,
> Which with distinct pre-eminence retain
> A fructifying virtue, whence, depress'd
> In trivial occupations, and the round
> Of ordinary intercourse, our minds –
> Especially the imaginative power –
> Are nourished and invisibly repair'd . . .
> Such moments chiefly seem to have their date
> From our first childhood

All this does not mean that he was static there amidst the first memories of an idyllic boyhood. Far from it, it was simply for him the starting-point and an ever refreshing well of early experience. It is no accident that there are similarities between *Highland River*, his sixth novel, and *The Atom of Delight*, his last work.

I now ponder on why he used to ask me about Turgenev, one of my favourite Russian authors. Turgenev, like Gunn, writes most exquisitely and sensitively about his native landscape and never more eloquently than when abroad during his periods of exile. Gunn, too, experienced his periods of exile but only in the characters of such books as *The Drinking Well* and *Wild Geese Overhead*. Could it have just been one lyrical writer admiring another, or was it the charm and force of Turgenev's heroines that had made an impact on my uncle? On both counts, there is something here for which the writers share an admiration: the beauty of nature and the strength and mystical appeal of women within the order of things.

On my return from a period of service at the embassy in Moscow in 1967 I found my uncle fascinated by my experiences there. He was always conscious of the failure of an experiment that had promised so much. Prince Kropotkin, the benevolent anarchist, was a figure well known to him and for whom he had respect. The danger of ideas gone wrong and bereft of the warmth of human experience worried him. He was to tell me that *Darkness at Noon*, written by Arthur Koestler in the 1930s, had terrified him in a way that few books had ever done. The most fearful feature of the book was its description of psychological torture of prisoners, this assault on the inner self.

This was not the first time that my uncle had come to grips with this intrusion into the innermost circle of being. In *Highland River* the last meeting between my father and his older brother Ben on the Western Front describes in the most chilling way the breakdown of the human psyche. The older brother, called Angus in *Highland River*, is seen by Kenn, my father, as a shell of what he had been. The horror of war had taken its toll. Ben's mannerisms were there but the inner being had gone. After a chat about old times in the village of their childhood and that Highland river of theirs the two boys became silent. 'And once Angus [Ben] looked about him with a sudden start as if in the short absence of thought something might have crept nearer. For there was no reality in the river. There was no reality outside the world in which he was.' My uncle accepted this as one of the most horrible side-effects of war. What frightened him more about *Darkness at Noon* was that the damage inflicted on the inner core was planned.

To exorcize this thought, at least partially, he wrote that most extraordinary of books, that anti-Utopian novel of the genre of *Brave New World*, *Nineteen Eighty-Four* and *Animal Farm*, *The Green Isle of the Great Deep*. It was also his riposte to the jibe that his writings had little relevance to the problems of the contemporary world. It would have cheered, if not amused, him to know that the great Jung himself had read this novel with profound interest. In a recent letter to me Jung's grandson writes:

My grandfather, C.J. Jung, read the above-mentioned book and was very impressed by this magical tale with its unfathomable thoughtful-ness. He worked on the unconscious and on the idea of archetypes, and obviously Neil Gunn's book is full of such mythical images and other archetypal symbols. Surely this tale must have been a vision or a really big dream of Neil Gunn's? My grandfather had the highest esteem for the book and wanted one of his pupils to work out an analysis of the archetypal contents.

My uncle's fascination with Zen Buddhism in his later years is well known. What excited him particularly was that many of the ideas within Eastern philosophy seemed already familiar to him. The converse was equally true. Professor Nakamura of Tokyo University was to write that many of my uncle's descriptions and observations had a direct relevance to his own childhood. The spiritual side of things was always important to my uncle. Although not a churchgoer or an adherent of conventional Christianity, he was never sceptical about Christ's contribution to the spiritual development of the world. Indeed, he was most interested in certain aspects of Christ's life and teachings. I remember once waiting with him to hear a radio programme called *The Silences of Christ*. We talked about the famous passage in St John's gospel when an adulteress had been brought to Christ by the scribes and Pharisees, who wished to know his views on a suitable punishment. 'But Jesus stooped down, and with his finger wrote on the ground, as though he had heard them not.' When the broadcast began it quickly became apparent that the speaker was off on a completely different tack – nothing to do with silences that go beyond words. 'He's missed the point,' was my uncle's laconic observation.

In his spiritual autobiography *The Atom of Delight* my uncle mentions L. H. Myers's book, *The Near and the Far*, and the interest he had in those passages marked in pencil by Daisy, to whom he had given the book as a gift. Two passages marked by Daisy seem to reflect my uncle's drift of thought at that time. The first concerns Christianity. 'To her he would often maintain with uncompromising rigour that the tendency of Christianity was to exalt the idea of social duty at the expense of the ideal of self-illumination.' The second is in the form of an exchange of views between teacher and pupil, with the pupil beginning the dialogue:

'In that state subject and object are one; awareness reflects awareness like two mirrors placed opposite, and that unity in duality seems to constitute self-consciousness, which is also selfhood.'

'The attribution of selfhood is unjustified.'

'But self-consciousness is selfhood. It is a closed circuit.'

'Pure consciousness is consciousness of itself, which is not the same as consciousness of one's self. Where there is no remembering personality, there can be no selfhood.'

If this appears esoteric stuff, I would suggest that my uncle had the gift of making forays into the world of philosophy a fascinating experience. 'To be "on the way" is to have an idea of what Eastern thought calls the Way . . . What happens by the way is not a matter of philosophy but of life, of universal experience.' And back to that wonderful start to *The Atom of Delight*: 'Often when looking for a thing, I find something else.'

Friends were important to my uncle and nothing hurt him more than the cessation of friendship for reasons outwith his control. One of his early literary friends had turned against him and this rejection left him with a sense of betrayal and sadness. This, added to the neglect of his books, particularly his later books, however, did not make him bitter, but rather more philosophical. Fortunately, he had made many new friends in his declining years, including his biographers-to-be, John Pick and Francis Hart. Such people were of immense encouragement to him, as indeed were his correspondence with Professor Nakamura and the high assessment of his place in Scottish literature by the German Kurt Wittig. But there were other believers in his value as a writer. It fell to my lot to read out (and answer) the many letters he received from people in this country and abroad for whom Neil's work had meant something. Many of these letters from schoolmasters, Anglican clergymen, restaurant owners, garage mechanics and students contained quotations from his work. 'Did I really write that?' he would say, quietly delighted by this genuine love of his writing. This was the natural response of a man for whom each book had been a new beginning. After all, in that long writing life there are always the unmistakable signs of the hunter at work, and for the hunter every day presents a fresh start. To be successful in his essential quest for self-illumination he had to exorcize some of the obstacles to his creativity. In human terms, the obstacles took the form of unsympathetic strangers. Colonel Hicks in *The Lost Glen* is the prototype for such people, a prime example of a negative and evil force at work.

Twenty-five years later in his last novel, *The Other Landscape*, my uncle has come to terms with the unsympathetic stranger, this time the Major, and makes him vanish in a cloud of humour. From time to time I used to tease my uncle about his choice of intruder, reminding him of a naval captain and colonel who were avid readers of his work. My description of a one-eyed Irish colonel, with whom I had a tot of rum and a long discussion on the early books in the midst of the Malayan jungle amused him – and, undoubtedly, pleased him. He admitted that he had chosen an easily identifiable group of people, military-cum-diplomatic types, to represent those who refused or were unwilling to be receptive to the needs or charm of a community for reasons of intellectual arrogance or a misplaced idea of caste. In their delicate and subtle biography, *Neil M. Gunn: A Highland Life*, Francis Hart and John Pick sum up my uncle's final triumph over the obstacles in his way. 'But he did not write *The Other Landscape* "to put the Major in his place". He wrote it to explore the mysteries of death, evil, misfortune and delight. It is beautiful, sombre, alive and positive, wildly ambitious and strangely youthful.'

Certainly the epithet youthful could always be applied to my uncle. For him walking was not just a form of exercise: it was a salute to the day, an opportunity to be in the landscape he loved. In his declining years he had a box placed near the entrance gate to the drive at Dalcraig as a precaution against premature tiredness; good neighbours on the road to North Kessock had made the offer of a perpetual staging-post, should the need be there, for a short rest, and a dram. These walks were part of him and I cannot but imagine him against a background of sea and hill – an integral part of the landscape to which he belonged. No book describes my uncle's delight in walking and taking in the landscape more than *The Well at the World's End*. There is no doubt that Peter Munro is my uncle himself and Fand his wife Daisy. The inscription on Daisy's copy says it all: 'This is Fand's own copy from her husband.' They are at the well and Peter says:

'At first I laughed. That there should have been water in the well when we were so certain it was dry! Water so clear we thought it wasn't there! Then – all at once – the queer feeling came over me that we were at the beginning of an adventure – setting out to find the – the something in life that we think isn't there.'

'You have long been wanting to do that,' she said.
'Do what?'
'Go away and find the well at the world's end.'
And he went.

When my uncle died, I was based near Edinburgh and was able to attend his funeral. In my letters to Francis Hart, one of his biographers-to-be and a great friend, I wrote:

The day of the funeral was one of those perfect northern days . . . The sky was cloudless and there was no wind. The ground was white with hoar frost. At the cemetery high above Dingwall one could see through the leafless trees to the hill and moor country near Braefarm House, where he had written so many of his books. We buried him to the cries of rooks in the bare branches. The mourners were all good friends. They included people like John Pick, Neil Paterson, Ronald Mavor, Finlay Macdonald and Ian Grimble. The Gunns present were able to treat them to a lunch in the National Hotel at Dingwall . . . The atmosphere was relaxed and happy but inevitably there was an undertone of sadness. We all felt we had to be cheerful in honour of him. He would have wanted it that way.

AT THE END OF THE DAY

AT THE END OF THE DAY

Francis Russell Hart

Hingham,
Massachusetts
June 1990

Dear Dairmid,

Many thanks for trusting me to go my own way in this centennial essay. Often in the past I have written about Neil according to one formal, impersonal plan or another. The modernist in Neil himself often paid homage to the belief that art should rise to the impersonal. When it comes to commentary, however, I am beyond such a belief. Personality is inescapable. In this first chance to write personally, I find it natural to talk in letters to you and three other friends, but I hope you won't mind if I talk through you to his as yet unknown future friends.

I want to explore a number of things, and to speak in my own voice, that of an old teacher whose only goal is to hand on Neil and his books to future readers. Handing on was what Neil did to me, and it is what happens in my favourites, *Bloodhunt* and *Young Art and Old Hector*. That wisest of teachers, Old Hector, knew at least one essential secret of teaching: our job is not to transmit our conclusions, but, rather, to introduce, guide, raise questions for students to answer in their own ways. I'll follow his lead.

Usually, when writing about Neil, I was speaking as a foreigner to other foreign readers who did not yet know him, and I was asked,

'Whom is he like? Where does he fit in?' I tried to answer with contexts. Now I want to try a very different answer: he is 'like himself'. But what is that? What are the essentials – which books, which qualities? This is not the same as the question I find tiresome and irrelevant: 'Which are his "greatest" or "best" books?' Essentials make fewer claims to canonical status; they may be far more intimate in value. So here I am on my own quest for essentials, and I expect to be surprised.

Like any true quest, like Peter Munro's in *The Well at the World's End*, this one will be full of accidents. Accidents can reveal essences. My own slow history of discovering Neil and his novels was a trail of accidents, and it may be worthwhile to recall a few of them and what they revealed. As I began discovering and 'interpreting' his books in an accidental sequence, I would write to him on each occasion, and he would respond, always with encouragement, sometimes satisfaction, sometimes puzzlement. He was then in his seventies, had long since stopped writing, felt remote from his novels. His kindness forced him back to them, and he could review them only in the copies he had religiously inscribed and presented to Daisy, his wife. She had been the chief repository of his writing, as she had been the person who typed his drafts – as Lorena edits mine, including these letters – the first person to whom they were given to read. Did he, like Menzies in *The Other Landscape*, write for her? How important this daily transaction must have been! This sense of first reader, of transmitter of his text! I came too late to see them together, and this would remain a block in my access to his writing. But it leads to an important question for some future student.

No writer works in a void; every writer writes in an immediate context, with a sense of audience, of primary readership, and this has an impact on his writing. Daisy must have been a part of his sense. But since Neil was a writer who wrote to be published and saw no point in writing otherwise, publishers were also of fundamental importance. We know the vexed history of his transactions with publishers, and how he fretted and manoeuvred over what they expected or what he thought they expected. Then, too, he had to cultivate and keep a reading public. This must have been tricky for one who started as an active Scottish nationalist, writing to a potential national audience, but also speaking for a new Scottish consciousness to an international readership, through the problematic mediation of foreign critical institutions. At midpoint in his career, that commitment faded, and so his sense of himself as a writer must have altered. A future student should explore the influence on his art of this evolving sense of audience.

A related question concerns his changing affiliations with other writers. First came the close alliance with Maurice Walsh; without it, Neil might never have become a novelist at all. Writing was a function of that companionship, and companionship would remain an essential condition of writing. Then followed the short alliance with Grieve and other young nationalists. For one who valued comradeship so highly, the betrayal of that bond must have had lasting impact. Alliances followed with John Macnair Reid, and with Edwin Muir and others sharply divided from the Grieve circle, and warm friendships with two remarkable women writers, Nan Shepherd and Naomi Mitchison. After the war came the close friendship with John Pick. My list is selective. My question is this: if these strong and shifting alliances were of essential importance to his sense of himself as a writer, what effects did they have on his writing? Even his dedications are not to be overlooked.

A third dimension of this approach is the complex question of 'influences'. Old-fashioned 'influence' study was often a bore, but the elusive fact remains: no writer begins and carries on without some sense of affiliation with, even dependence on, earlier writers – though it sometimes operates as a rejection. In my experience, Neil was always inclined to disclaim influences. For one thing, he held to a firm faith in originality. For another, he believed in sticking close to his own experiences. The influences he did acknowledge were non-literary, reflecting a characteristic scepticism about 'lit'ry gents' and institutions. The only 'lit'ry' influence he and I ever chatted whimsically about was his putative 'love affair' with Fiona Macleod. He was able to joke with me about it, for he knew it did not embarrass me and need not embarrass him in my company. But what a long, painful struggle he had with those who refused to absolve him of 'Celtic mysticism', a charge I have never been able to understand.

It takes me back to that first accident on my own trail. My university library had one Gunn novel, so it became the first I read: *The Lost Glen*. What it meant to 'discover' Neil in that book I'll speak about in my second letter. Suffice to say, that initial exposure to an ornate Celtic fatalism had a disproportionate and distorting impact on one who was as yet merely a romantic tourist to 'ben and glen'. A few months later, as a Fulbright Fellow in Edinburgh, I was taken to Alex Frizzell's bookshop. Representing Neil on the shelves were later novels, from *The Green Isle of the Great Deep* to *Bloodhunt*. Thus, my reading jumped from *The Lost Glen* directly to a radically different fictional world, and I discovered with uncritical exhilaration that Neil was an intellectually complex 'modern'.

The third accident was academic. A friendly senior colleague popped into my office to announce that he was arranging a 'panel' on anti-Utopian fiction for a convention. 'Oh!' said I, 'I've just read a wonderful anti-Utopian novel.' He had never heard of Neil or *The Green Isle of the Great Deep*, but in the kindly spirit of Old Hector, he suggested I give a paper. The paper was presented, and I took the brave step of sending a copy to the author. He replied in some amazement but with warmth, too tactful to express uneasiness at being linked to Huxley, Orwell, and Zamyatin, or being used as a socialist corrective. The result was a correspondence which had the accidental effect of placing this book at the centre of my sense of Neil's fiction. If I say little about it in these letters, it is because I am seeking essentials elsewhere, not because I question that book's pre-eminence.

Shortly thereafter, we had a house visit from a Burns scholar, Ross Roy, who was canvassing the sparse world of American 'Scots' scholars to support a new journal, and would I contribute an article to the opener? Another grand chance to raise a large claim on Neil's behalf before ignorant America! I thought Neil would be pleased; I was now writing to him when I wrote about him. The novels this time were *The Key of the Chest*, *The Shadow* and *Bloodhunt*; my shock title was 'Neil Gunn's Fiction of Violence'. This anti-regionalist took the violence of the whole modern world for his subject and gave it the most complex intellectual scrutiny, about which a young academic critic could discourse ad infinitum. What else were serious novels for? You see, by accident I had begun with complexity – complexity was the darling of critics then – and would take years to work my way through to simplicity. Future students, I hope, will start out free of this trap. Simplicity is the most elusive quality for many moderns to discover, trust and value.

My title evoked some playful uneasiness in Neil: a gentle, peaceable man a writer of violence? Here began one continuous thread in our correspondence. I would pop forth with some such scheme, and he would express pleasure, and at the same time, hint that I had not got it 'quite right'. My efforts to find out how I was 'off' brought elusive answers, sometimes the stance or strategy of 'elusiveness', the mask of the shy, private Highlander. Were we playing the game of master and disciple in his beloved *Zen in the Art of Archery*? Were my academic formulations violating some deeply private sense of his books? His commitment to privacy operates as an essential strategy of his books. Privacy is complicated.

Let me describe one delicate aspect of our relationship and what it taught me. I had long been interested in the making of biography. Because of the wonderful accident whereby a foreign disciple and his wife could pay long visits to Neil in his Black Isle solitude, I let myself slip into the biographical role. I interviewed him, slipped up to the guest-room to scribble all I could retain, plagued him with letters of enquiry. I should have realized that these were often tiring, sometimes unnerving invasions of his privacy. He played a necessary game of response: he struggled to remember and transmit; he retreated into elusive uncertainties. I should have understood. He had the artist's essential desire to retain possession of his own intimate sense of remembered experiences. He had done so throughout his imaginative life, and had climaxed that life with one of the most elusive, tranformative of autobiographies. In *The Atom of Delight*, he had given his own ultimate shape and texture to his remembered life, and here was I, a stubbornly curious, matter-of-fact Other, trying to unmake that mythic construct. I use 'mythic' in its true neutral sense; every autobiography must be mythic.

These invasions were put to the test when he was weak and ill. Scott and Gifford asked for a 'short' biographical introduction to their collection *Neil M. Gunn: The Man and the Writer* (1973). My draft went to Neil for correcting and monitoring, to be read to him by brother John, and you, Dairmid, with responses sent to me. The most revealing response was a passage written by himself in his own hand to be inserted as if written by me. It recounted the 1937 episode of giving up home, society, security to be 'off and away' with his wife to the Western Isles and Brae. This was the life-passage which had most preoccupied him in our talks, and he could allow no one else to write it, to get it just right. It appears at the bottom of page 43 in Scott and Gifford. Future students will miss some essentials if they do not grasp its profound importance to him.

One other incident was revealing in the same way. I had slipped naïvely into the folly of projecting a great grey tome on the novel and Scotland. Neil aided and abetted my presumption. My struggle for structure called for a chapter on 'The Novel of the Highlands', and, since Highland writers had identified the Clearances as the pivotal event of modern Highland history, I drafted a comparison of a few Clearance novels. The draft as usual went to Neil, and his painstaking comments did not hide some agitation. I had not got it quite right; the same was true of the other novelists. I did not realize for years how painfully possessive a subject that had to be for a Sutherlander – and Neil was a Sutherlander.

Eventually I read the interview with George Bruce where Neil spoke of the shame 'of the thing'.

'Why should you feel ashamed?'

'Because our own people did it.'

In a letter to Agnes Mure Mackenzie he wrote, 'There was a double betrayal, far ben in the spirit.' With such guides, one begins to hear those words 'shame' and 'betrayal' echoing in the novels, and to link them with privacy, with secrecy as a condition of spiritual survival.

But not till writing this to you did accident take me back to a forgotten passage by the social theorist Georg Simmel, writing of the fascinations of secrecy as an essential condition of human interaction:

> These attractions of secrecy are related to those of its logical opposite betrayal . . . The secret, too, is full of the conviction that it can be betrayed; that one holds the power of surprises, turns of fate, joy, destruction – if only, perhaps, of self-destruction. For this reason, the secret is surrounded by the possibility and temptation of betrayal; and the external danger of being discovered is interwoven with the internal danger, which is like the fascination of the abyss, of giving oneself away.

In a world of betrayal, secrecy is the only counterforce. I leave it to some future student to follow the implications.

Another kind of student could pursue privacy in a more 'lit'ry' direction. When I taught in Virginia, our department had the pleasant chore of offering weekly literary readings to the public. My turn came, and again I grabbed the occasion to introduce Neil. I selected a few fine set pieces: the cliff-climbing from *The Silver Darlings*, the walk of the Royal Mile from *The Drinking Well*, the myth of God and the old woman from *Highland River*, and so on. I pulled out the histrionic stops, and what was heard was fine public rhetoric, a totally misleading introduction to a writer of such intimacy, such delicate interiority. Not much later, in Edinburgh at Festival time, my friends Ian and Meta Gilmour invited me to work up a dramatized selection of the two novelists I knew best, Scott and Gunn. Neil seemed pleasantly amused at finding himself in the company of the Great Scot, but what a misleading conjunction! Scott was a dramatic novelist, working from the models of his beloved dramatists. Neil was not. His voices are private and intimate, and when a 'public voice' breaks out occasionally in his novels, it is a violation or a detour.

Perhaps this is why a truly appropriate filmic version of that intimately intersubjective novel, *The Silver Darlings*, could not be made, or why, when Neil did write a novel intended for filming, *The Drinking Well*, it lacked his essential qualities. In skilled and sensitive hands, *The Well at the World's End* and *Bloodhunt* were successfully adapted to dramatic form. But these late novels are quite different; the boundary between 'private' and 'public' had dissolved into something else. Neil's sense of the novel had changed, and his norm had moved closer to the communal voice of the storyteller. The Spanish critic Savater suggests beautifully what I have in mind for some future student of voice to explore:

> A story can always be read aloud, indeed there is no other way to read it. In the novel, the book is a hiding place and the scene of a withdrawal; a solitude has sought to nestle in the inviolable silence of its pages. The contents of a novel cannot really be told by voice, while all stories, even when read alone, are really being told in living words . . . The birthplace of the novel is the solitary individual . . . Storytelling demands a community in order to exist.

If he is right, then Neil's changing narrative voices – which no one, I think, has yet studied – are inseparable from his evolving beliefs in community.

At any rate, Dairmid, you now have a glimpse of what I want to do. I hope I can frame some questions of use to Neil's future students, for in their hands, not in the old hands joined in this collection, his future lies. Our job is, like Old Hector's, simply to hand on. The teaching job I have most often been asked to do is the first and most important: to introduce; to offer advice on where and how to begin. Beginnings shape all that follows. Becoming a little notorious in a world remote from Neil Gunn's country as a fellow who wrote about someone named Gunn, I have repeatedly been asked by colleagues, students, friends, even relatives, 'Where do I begin?' 'Where do I go next?' For instance, just the other week an older relative, Cleveland Gilcreast, phoned me. He had read John's and my biography, and in his town library he had found a single Gunn novel: *The Silver Bough*! He liked it. What next?

Dear Cleve,

Your phone call caught me by surprise! The most challenging question I'm ever asked about Neil is how best to be introduced to his books. By accident, you phoned just as I was fretting over whether I had anything new and useful to say for his centenary. You gave me one answer. What I say or think no longer matters much. What matters is who reads Neil from now on, and what essential things make them glad to do so.

What might one find in reading *The Silver Bough* first? The last time I read it, I read so fast and with such enjoyment, that I didn't pause for thought until around page 200. How, you must have asked yourself, could a novelist make such sparkling farce, such 'silent and delicious mockery', out of an archaeological dig, out of finding and losing a golden crock, out of a local thieving idiot? And why combine this 'bony' comedy with the unearthed horror story of jungle warfare and the painful healing of its protagonist? Neil's publisher tried to find a logical answer, 'some deep inner connection', and, missing it, thought he had missed something 'essential', Neil had proved himself such a fine craftsman of intricate connections that the expectation was natural. Perhaps Neil no longer believed in such connectedness.

Perhaps *you* simply accepted some bewilderment as part of the game Neil was playing, and if so, good for you! I often have to advise serious students: you'll be far better off if you stop trying so hard to 'understand', for the effort often obstructs discovery of what is essential.

You were meeting Neil at the final stage of his writing, the start of the Cold War, when he was horrified at where the world was heading, and was trying to master his horror by a healing humour and whimsy. If he could keep himself whole, perhaps he could do the same for others, as he did for me. He was also testing his faith, both artistic and social, that all human stories come together in one story, the essential story of joy in moments of living, and of the rebirth of compassion and community. He was burdened much of his life with a sense of the tragedy of the modern world, but increasingly he was bent on sharing a healing intuition of some light beyond the darkness. His negative critics never stopped calling this 'escapism', and he never stopped trying to explain that some 'escapist' impulses are legitimate, life-giving. I like what the Spanish writer Savater says: 'We raise like a banner the word that for some is censure, for others an incentive, and for everyone a proper defence against the fatal poison of nostalgia: escape. But, all of a sudden, escape from what, and to go where?' That is the real question.

If you are interested in that question, you might want to read a very different novel of ten years before. The hero of *Wild Geese Overhead*, a young Glasgow journalist, carries his 'escapist' – that is, life-giving – intuitions of rural, natural life into the violence and degradation of city slums. His socialist friends accuse him of 'escapism'; he argues with them; he gets humanly involved with city poor, and almost gets killed on city streets; he finds love and survival – they go together in essential Gunn – at the end. Or you might go next to a novel three years later than *The Silver Bough*, a novel about a temporary escape. I don't mean to get stuck on this 'issue', but it haunted Neil, and his future readers will want to think carefully about it.

Having suggested this later book, *The Well at the World's End*, I thought I had better reread it myself, so I did. In it, I felt closest to the Neil I knew, but you didn't know him. Nowhere is Neil more at home with or closer to his central figure. When there is irony, it is Peter-Neil laughing at himself. When the author portrays Peter's thoughts and feelings, you cannot find the line between author and Peter. Peter combines two sides of Neil: the speculative man – Peter is a history professor – and the practical countryman – Peter is son of a famous shepherd. And the episodes come, more than in any other book, from Neil's own, or someone else's, true adventures.

Adventures they are, too. The middle-aged professor, on a holiday walking tour away from his wife, goes in search of 'something' that seems 'nothing', not the legendary 'well at the world's end', but the living water in it, the water you cannot see but can touch. Is there truth, real water, in the so-called illusions of ordinary people? He wants to find out, and he is led to the adventures. Since Neil knows what true adventure is, Peter never knows what will come next, but he is *open* to it, and that is the key to reading the book, too: stay open; be surprised; take events as they come. Nothing is fated here; fate is a contrivance. In an open universe, says William James, chance or accident rules, and the result is freedom. Neil was a skilful contriver of plots, and a reader can enjoy the craft, but here he takes a holiday from contrivance. I am taking a holiday in these letters, and I am tempted to take this book as my model, but I may, like Peter, get lost, lose control. (So what? Lorena asks me.)

For the first half of the book, 'So what?' is my motto. The adventures follow easefully with always a sense of new revelation, of 'quiet wonder' at the smallest thing. Thought is 'no more than the scent of a flower', the same kind of reality as the suspended drop on the tip of an old woman's nose as she pours tea. I walk with Peter the boundary where image, sensation, revelation are one, and where menace and delight easily slip into each other. Through the visit to the old woman, through the terrible ghost prank at the haunted cottage, the night-time knock-out and orgy with the illegal whisky-makers, even through the weird woodland lost-and-found paradise with Cocklebuster and his bewitched dog – all through these, I too am bewitched. Then something happens.

'I *loved* Cocklebuster,' Neil chortled once. And I get the feeling often of the author's real love for these characters, especially for Peter's wife Fand, Neil's wife Daisy. This may be why they seem so unusually free, so independent of authorial control, so unpredictable like Peter's adventures.

Did Neil love Cocklebuster too much? Once Cocklebuster gets

talking, his metaphysical gyrations take over, even take over Peter's mind (Neil's mind). Peter is divided into the speculative self he has been running away from, and the 'wild man' of instinct he feels driven to seek and identify with. But Neil's idea of a true holiday includes Cocklebuster's blether. If Shakespeare's 'Dalilah' was punning, Neil's was metaphysical blether, and if you really want to know him, here is one of his essential delights.

But you can sense that it eventually puts him on the defensive by the way he contrives to jar Peter back to ordinary, brutal reality with the street violence and the coastal rescue tale. And when Peter begins repeatedly trying to sum up all his adventures, to pull them all together and 'plot' them in reverse, I suspect Neil is trying to assuage the bewilderment his publisher felt. Or perhaps he himself has grown uneasy with his freedom, and as a result, he now seems out of control.

But this is one of the risks of storytelling. After all, Odysseus and Scheherazade told stories to survive, and why be surprised if they sometimes lost control? It occurs to me that if you want to know an author, you need to meet him sometimes when he is out of control. Every true author has to walk the boundary between freedom and control, and we should walk it with him. Come to think of it, I first met Neil on that boundary more than thirty-five years ago. Like you, I picked up the only one of his novels in 'my' library, the second he wrote, *The Lost Glen*. No book could seem more different than *The Well* and *The Silver Bough*. I wonder whether, if you read it now, you would catch anything essential that it shares with them. Inspired by your first exposure via *The Silver Bough*, I decided to try to recapture my own, so I reread it. Here is what happened, in the novel, and in me.

A young Highlander has left his poverty-stricken grey coast to 'make it' into the ministry via the university. He is caught in an innocent-enough party brawl in his lodgings by his puritanical uncle, goes home a 'failure', and here he also fails to save his fisher-father in a storm. This is a book about failing to save people, so different from *The Silver Bough* and *The Well* with their climactic salvations, but the issue is the same: can people be saved? Young Ewan declines into the life of a 'gillie', servile fishing guide to tourists. No figure so haunted Neil's negative imagination as the gillie, epitome of a culture robbed of its *raison d'être*. Ewan's spiritual aspirations decline into dark, bitter fatalism. The story follows his conflicts, racial and sexual rivalries, with the head resident tourist, retired Colonel Hicks. 'Fate' or 'chance' – Neil seems uncertain which – draws them together at the stormy climax. Ewan kills the colonel and then himself.

It is always risky to summarize someone else's complex story. When I teach a book, I offer my own summary and ask students to correct and revise it. As we argue over 'what happens', we find we are actually exploring what happens to *us* as we read. As for me, reluctance made me want to scan *The Lost Glen*, keep my distance, but I could not. It is a novel of absorption, obsession really, with none of the distancing whimsy of *The Silver Bough*. I become absorbed because the author is, as he moves in slow rhythm among three consciousnesses, Ewan, Hicks, and Hicks's niece Claire. The outer world has ceased to matter; this human place has lost its reality with its spirit and is merely a setting for battles within. You would sorely miss Neil's delicate, sensuous rendition of the outer world, human and natural, as you saw it in *The Silver Bough*, or as you would find it, say, in the lovely novel he wrote to pull himself out of the 'lost glen', *Morning Tide*. Public life has been corroded, and private life survives only in secret gloom. The only living vision is Claire's, but Claire is helpless to prevent the tragedy and can only look on in futile, sometimes angry compassion. The author does, too. Here, as in some other books, Neil projects his own positive vision through a woman character.

Hicks is one of the ugliest versions of what Neil would repeatedly conceive of as human evil. Some future student should explore Neil's 'destroyers' and what he believed, not just about what evil is, but why it is, and when it is beyond redemption. You've got a head start with the victim Martin in *The Silver Bough*. A student more politically inclined should look at such figures as images of negative authority, one of Neil's persistent concerns. Positive authority is hard to find in his books: influence, yes; power, no.

In this early book, Neil already had a power of his own: architectonic power, the craft of building diverse elements into an integrated design. Too little attention has been paid to his narrative craft. But always, for the story-architect, there is the key question of where it all leads, how it will end. An author's 'sense of an ending' tells most about his vision of the human story. In *The Lost Glen*, the catastrophe is both 'accidental' and 'fated'. If it had to happen, why?

What did fatality mean to Neil? In later novels, he was for ever struggling against fatalism, and *The Lost Glen* is a fascinating point of departure. He believed in 'happy endings', but a revealing hint in his last novel, *The Other Landscape*, suggests that the author felt guilty striving for them. Why feel guilty? Why keep striving then? *There's* a subject for study. Revisit the gloriously happy ending of *The Silver Bough*, or the barely averted disaster of *The Well*. *Butcher's Broom* ends half tragically, and *The Serpent* 'ends' tragically, then transcends that ending. Happy endings are sometimes uncertain, as in *The Key of the Chest*, *The Shadow*, and the three part-endings of *Morning Tide*. In *The Lost Glen* there is no struggle.

At any rate, all this speculation lay far in the future when I first read it, an uninitiated romantic charmed by 'Celtic gloom'. So, leaving you alone, Cleve, I'll turn to the company of another fellow, one who has tactfully guided me over the years. John Pick took over this role when Neil died, and without him, I'd have little to say, and almost no one to talk to, about Neil.

Dear John,

Many thanks, as always, for your good advice. When I wrote you in something of a panic, you suggested I follow my nose and chase down personal responses to some of Neil's more puzzling books. As you see, I am on my own quest. But, given our years of talking together about Neil, I must write you about two books I feel reluctant to return to. I hope to understand this reluctance, perhaps overcome it. Every quest has its risky, even negative stages. Will I miss the essentials here? If so, will I at least know better what they are?

With *Highland River*, I feel a strong obligation to overcome my reluctance. This was a pivotal book, a prize-winner, which so impressed publisher and public as to strengthen Neil's confidence and give him the wherewithal to continue. It is his most sophisticated experiment in modernist form, and I delight in its intricate artistry. Someone some day will write *The Craft of Gunn*; he took pleasure and pride in craft, celebrated it in his novels, and was, as we know, an astute critic of craft in others. Why, then, did he give up modernist form? One possible answer: when Virginia Woolf and her contemporaries transformed the novel, they discounted and moved away from 'story', from narrative itself, in the direction of 'lyric' or poem. Neil, as he rediscovered at the time of *The Silver Darlings*, found the source of narrative genius in traditional story. Paradoxically, more than any other book, *Highland River* seeks sources of art that are remote from his own cultural tradition.

The mode of the book sets it apart from the rest, except for *The Serpent*, its nearest kin. Its mode is memory; in a sense, its subject is memory, for the entire action is remembered, just as in a different way, old Tom's past is all recaptured in his present. In *Highland River*, what matters is what is 'memorable', and the memorable can only be recaptured – as for Wordsworth – by a later interpretative memory. The original experience is merely a 'source'. Source of what? Clearly a philosophy. Neil confessed to his publishers that he had reached a stage at which he had 'something to say' of a philosophical nature, and might get into trouble making a novel say it. How well can a novel serve as such an instrument? Sometimes well, as when the philosophy is embodied in fable as in the Art and Hector books, or in open quest, as in *The Well at the World's End*, or in the spiritual *Bildungsroman*, *The Serpent*. Less so, perhaps, when the novel turns argumentative, as when Kenn tackles his 'multiple disputant', or has his 'urge to be explicit, even to labour, what is infinitely elusive'. I know why Neil felt defensive about his views of 'golden age', 'secretiveness', 'escape', but I regret it when argument displaces narrative, the result being what Kenn calls 'all that fine rhetoric'. And it *is*.

For those like us interested in the substance of the argument, *Highland River* is crucial. It first articulates what would become his philosophical anarchism, yet in this it is curious. Anarchism envisions the individual in community. Here, the boy grows up in a certain kind of community, but his growth is essentially an escape from community, a growth towards isolated individuality. The community Kenn finally identifies with is an abstraction called 'the folk'. In *The Serpent*, which I have just reread, the emphasis on individuality is equally strong, but community is inseparable from it.

Highland River as a novel once more did not hold my interest – in this respect it is unique among Neil's books. I found myself skimming some of the long episodes of fish-bashing and rabbit-trapping, knowing that male readers of the 1930s enjoyed them. At the end of the day, I happened to hear an interview with that fine woman science-

historian, Evelyn Fox Keller, on gender in science, and it suddenly
struck me how exclusively male a book this is. The archetype of the
growth of the male, hunter, scientist, individualist, is in control, as
nowhere else in Neil. Woman exists only in the generic mother, shut
out of the male world, living contentedly as servant and caretaker.
Kenn, a very male scientist, grows by setting himself apart from family
and community in solitary dignity. (What an unusually solemn book
this is!) 'He was in complete command of the situation.' 'A man had
to hold himself with his solitary, lonely integrity.' Kenn confronts
nature to possess it. The river is *his* river, and because of his possessive
relationship to it, he can remain untouched by the modern world. His
river is not a source of insight into the world, but a protective armour
against it. The heroes of *Wild Geese Overhead* and *The Serpent* are
touched, are far more vulnerable, and grow in humanity as a result. In
Highland River, there is no feminine consciousness, perspective,
corrective – and all three have become for me essential parts of Neil's
imagination.

With this notion gnawing at me, I was astonished to reread *The
Serpent*. One of the chastening lessons I learned was the degree to
which accidents have distorted my earlier readings. Neil wrote me
that it was 'one of my own peculiar ones about which I'd say nowt', so
I felt compelled to seek personal matters. Biographical bias focused my
attention on Neil's early intellectual history, so that I found the tragic
love-story irrelevant, and asked him why! Margaret's disclosures in
1978 led us to focus instead on that story of secret love, so I slighted
the rest. This new reading was my first of the story *per se*, and I found
it compelling all the way!

It is certainly different. It seems his most consistently naturalistic;
its matter-of-fact, evocative style quite in keeping with Tom and his
life. Local reality prevails: the quarry 'lay at the base of the shoulder of
the hill to their left as they entered the Glen just after leaving the
village'. The hill, Tom's retreat, is a natural place; not possessed by
Tom, like Kenn's river, but possessive of him. The novel is rich in
'characters' and community. The dreadful, ill father has archetypal
power for Tom, but remains a pathetic old man. The mother is an
anxious, lonely woman. Janet, while a visionary figure for Tom, is an
ordinary, sensuous, fearful young woman. Tom, an intellectual, is also
a craftsman, lover, friend. The community is a persuasive mix of good

and bad, and individuals are of it: 'The living essence of the communal whole. The living individual.' As Tom tells the shepherd: 'Every personal problem is more than a personal problem; it is a communal one.' Tom sums all this up in the quietest, most naturalistic statement of theme in all of Neil's novels:

> For at the end of the day, what's all the bother about? Simply about human relations, about how we are to live one with another on the old earth. That's all, ultimately. To understand one another, and to understand what we can about the earth, and in the process gather some peace of mind and, with luck, a little delight.

This marvellous simplicity makes me eager to go back to *Young Art and Old Hector*, and to *Bloodhunt*, but not yet.

Whatever its argumentative origins, the book is not argumentative. Its creed is realized through Tom's experience, as he moves from freethinker, to proud sceptic, to a man chastened by love, community, the natural world. The remarkable final stage in his redemption is his changing intuition of women. It starts in distrust:

> A curious treachery there was in women; not so much treachery as a ruthlessness. They would lie, and deceive, and be treacherous to the utmost degree, in order to get their desire. As if their desire was something more than themselves and knew no law.

But he moves to a new understanding:

> He saw now how vivid a woman's apprehension of the real was. A man could cloud his apprehension with all sorts of rules, categories, principles, theories. Not so a woman. She saw what she wanted, the inner kernel, the thing-in-itself, and went, by some law of her feminine being, unerringly for that.

Tom is led to this revelation by his reading, by his discovery in Rousseau of 'the feminine mind', as opposed to the 'male categories, the philosophical absolutes, the masculine rules of life'. This is the only place I know of in Neil where he acknowledges that the 'feminine' is not necessarily a matter of gender.

But here, dear John, I am in deep water with the question of the 'feminine' in Neil's imagination. Begging your pardon, I should turn to another letter and talk to a reader better able to understand this aspect of Neil than you or I. If you saw and heard her, you would know she is true Irish. And if Neil had, he'd have burst into song, as he did with Lorena on 'Oh, what a beautiful morning!'

Dear Laura,

You were so kind and curious that I know you will remember 'Literature of Modern Scotland', our course in the 1980s, the only chance I ever had to teach what I had studied for so long. I wanted to 'hand it on' to a few young Americans like you. Besides, I knew I would not understand what I knew until I taught it. What might you all, knowing nothing to start, find in it? You were 'English majors', but many of you were Irish-Americans interested in Irish culture, so you met Scots as Celtic kin. Neil would have been pleased by that. Alas, he was long gone and I could not turn to him for wise counsel. Would you like him? I wondered nervously. We could read only one of Neil's books. Which would introduce him best? We read *The Silver Darlings*.

I had not wanted to choose that book. The 'reasons' are complex. You folks knew and cared nothing about 'critics' but they have tended to split into two camps: some prefer his early books, climaxing with this big 'historical novel', or 'folk epic'; others favour later, more 'complex' novels. By accident, my loyalties lay with the second camp. For good reasons, some accidental (cost, availability), we chose *The Silver Darlings* anyway, and I set out to rediscover it through your responses. You were bowled over by it, making it the high point of our course. I was, too.

Our enthusiasms differed. You all were fascinated by the book as a rich repository of history, culture, folklore. I wanted us to appreciate it as a work of art, beautifully patterned in interweaving rhythms, personal and communal, historical and psychological. We studied it in five 'movements': First Movement (chapters 1–3): beginnings; Second (chapters 4–9): six years of peace and growth; the strained triangle of mother-son-rival; Third (chapters 10–13): the 'plague' section; Finn's two trips; Fourth (chapters 14–18): away to fishing adventures in the west; Fifth (chapters 19–24): difficult conclusions. Our focus was on rhythm, and rhythm means variation in repetition, change in continuity. Of each movement, we asked: what is the same here? what is new? what is advanced or revealed, what repeated? Perhaps if some future readers would follow our tracks, they too would discover what a remarkable composition this is, what a lovely, intricate music. Music has to come before 'meaning'.

We looked closely at one chapter, the novel in epitome. Chapter 6, 'The Land and the Sea', is composed around two episodes, the cow in the corn and the boat in the storm. We explored their contrasts and tensions: past and future, the enduring and the changing, stasis and motion, woman and man, age and youth, authority and freedom, teaching and learning, tradition and experience, fear and delight, good and evil, individuality and community, all subtly woven together as implications of the two episodes. What superb craft!

I posed what is for me the climactic 'problem'. The final movement moves slowly through obscure, powerful disturbances and resistances in Finn: his restless voyages, his loves and jealousies, his searches for peace, his hidings and retreats from adult life. What is Finn's 'problem'? I asked. What is haunting and obstructing him? Why do pride, success, love leave him unsatisfied? What does he learn? There is no simple analytic answer. Our tentative answers went like this. Finn's final development parallels his mother's. The problem for both seems 'sexual', but is more. Neil often links sexuality with history; the real problem is the seductiveness of the past. We see now why the uncertainty of Tormad the father's death hangs over the whole story, for Tormad is the past, and the past must be let go of. Catrine finally accepts this, and so does Finn. He identifies with his father, yet feels he is his own father, has his own destiny, as Catrine does. What he learns in Uist, through story, dance, song, is that the past does not die; its essentials become timeless in art and ritual. Finn acquires the mastery of telling his own story, becomes his own author. But this final step to individuality brings him a sense of belonging to the whole community, the story as a whole.

We had discovered an extraordinary art-narrative, encompassing the most public and most intimate, its sheer narrative momentum, its interweaving of thematic implications. In these respects, it is excelled by none other of Neil's books. I might add that I now have only one worn copy, for I have given several away to other young readers, all of whom have reported back the same sense of awe and pleasure that you all felt.

But now let me raise two questions for readers like you, especially women. Neil came close to Joyce in his attitude towards history. For Joyce, history was 'nightmare'; for Neil, 'betrayal'. Yet, while he was bored by history in school and darkly sceptical of it later, he felt compelled to deal with it. When he addresses history on a large scale, in *The Silver Darlings*, but also in *Sun Circle*, *Butcher's Broom*, *The Drinking Well*, does history have a meaning for him, or is it merely a negative, possessive feeling? Specifically, the history of the Clearances, of which he said, 'I'd always felt the *need* to write . . . I hated doing it.' Yet he did it again and again. To understand his imagination is to come to terms with this compulsion.

The other question is related. His repeated theme is that history is male, and women are outside of, or behind, history. I can imagine some feminist readers deploring this as a male stereotype, but it is much more. For me, a male reader, one essential of Neil's imagination is its 'feminine' side. Before our course, I had never faced the question of women's responses to this male novelist.

In my grey tome on 'the Scottish novel', I tried to understand why, for many of these male novelists, the most significant central characters were women. It is as if, given the stoic intellectual culture that produced these men, the real liberating of imagination came through empathy with the feminine, an intuition of its entrapment, wisdom, compassion, anarchism. Look at Neil's first, *The Grey Coast*, and the young croft woman in her daily struggles with the mean oppressions of her uncle, the sexual menace of the farmer, the fatalistic weakness of her lover. Set her next to Catrine, to the independent and courageous Elie and Mairi in *Butcher's Broom*, to the comparable old-young women pair in *The Shadow*, much later, and so on. This pursuit I leave to you, for I feel too much the limitations of a male reader. Instead, I take us back to the intimate relationships closest to that old-young women bond. They, too, are beyond history and sexuality. In them, I hope to discover why the Gunn books I hold in most lasting affection are two that could hardly seem more different. I do not know whether they are his 'best' or 'greatest', though a case could be made for one of them. But 'greatness' is alien to what matters in *Bloodhunt* and *Young Art and Old Hector*. 'Goodness' is far less pretentious.

How different they are to read! I reread *Bloodhunt* non-stop, not wanting to pause for thought or notes. When I take notes, I find I have simply described its story, its movement, its ease of transition, natural accidents, effortless slips between taut suspense and comic conflict. I follow Sandy's sharply plotted actions so intensely that I find myself moving in his small, menaced world. Pauses for reflection are rare: 'It was not a thing of learning, of knowledge, that gripped at the heart.' The book is essentially 'gripping'. In *Young Art and Old Hector*, I enjoy my pauses, for each story has its own closure, proverbial crystallization, and I stop for a while to live with it. *Bloodhunt*, by contrast, is told in a terse, naturalistic style, pared down to the minimal things, barely spoken. I am struck by how few markings I have in my old copy – I am a disgraceful book marker – as if nothing called attention to itself as separate from the rest. Both books are free of the epic struggles and metaphysical gyrations of more ambitious novels. I value those essentials, but here I value constraint, smallness of scale, simplicity.

This is not the simplicity of innocence, of early awakening, but the final innocence reached only beyond complexity. Blake might call it the Higher Innocence, and here that is in a nutshell:

> On his way home, Sandy found himself sitting in the ditch by the roadside smiling. Beyond the trials and sins of the world, beyond police and dogma, beyond prayer and innocence – but no, not beyond innocence, for it was rare as innocence, this sitting in a ditch smiling, with the spirit rising on the air. If I can rise from the ditch myself, he thought, for the dram had rather gone to his feet, but just then he heard something coming, got up and took off his hat in so courteous a manner that the strange automobile, though gleaming with wealth, drew up to give the simple old countryman a lift.

And, of course, he *is* one – and he is not.

Repeatedly I have read this book with the same tension and astonishment, always ending with some shout such as, 'Bloody great masterpiece.' The book says it best: 'It was like a miracle, like a hidden pattern of events happening *quite simply* [my stress] within the large pattern that touched it everywhere yet remained unaware of it.' What it achieves in Sandy is a simplicity of vision so comprehensive that it easily reveals the largest of patterns in the smallest, not an other landscape, not a second sight, but a single landscape of vision at once human and transcendent. How does Neil manage this resonance with only the barest of hints? I suddenly worry. Perhaps I, the reader, am doing it, importing the universals of law and justice, the dilemmas of wisdom, old age's tension between death and life, the fatalistic peace of isolation against the dangerous love of community? I bring a store of memories of what such situations, figures, actions meant to Neil. For example, I know several novels in which the impulse to hide, to escape, is an explicit thematic issue. Here the impulse is simply an integral part of Sandy's age and life, and it is opposed, not by counter-argument, but by the instinctual demands of life in those he must help and protect. Likewise, while Sandy sees, feels, thinks things that Neil liked to see, feel, think, he does not serve as a spokesman for the author. He is a full, autonomous character, who reminds me most of Aunt Phemie in *The Shadow*.

You, Laura, may be interested in this. He is that rare thing, a believably good man. Yet, in Sandy more than any other figure in Gunn, we have a male character who has effectively assumed the traditional woman's role: the housekeeper, the practical caretaker, the instinctive protector against male categories of law and justice. To Alan the outcast killer, and later to Liz the pregnant girl, he is both paternal and maternal. For Liz, when her baby is born in his barn, he is the experienced good shepherd and the sure midwife. Yet, in his final choice to remain silent and end the cycle of justice, he is what he feels himself to be, the old man of the tribe.

Hector, too, is the old man of the tribe, cultivating and protecting new life. Hector, too, is the caretaker, less in Sandy's practical way, more as spiritual guide for whom 'wisdom' is all-important. What is wisdom? How to get it? Why is the wise man better than the hero? Wisdom is a domain outside of male categories such as the authority of law, a protection against that authority. Getting wisdom is as simple as sticking your thumb in your mouth, but so simple as to be hard won, especially if you are of the age of the 'fathers' in the middle years, who live in fear because they are so 'important'. What is 'important' is not what is essential. 'When men are full of importance women have to be full of sense.' But Hector is full of sense, which is part of wisdom. He likes his old age because 'now I know at last what is important and what is not.' He has replaced for Neil the archetypal figure of the mother. He is no archetype; he is a 'simple old countryman'.

Or am I growing sentimental? Is there something in me that responds too warmly, affectionately, to this goodness? Do I turn to fiction for escape from complexity and 'importance'? I suspect many of us do, and kid ourselves when we think otherwise. The book brings tears to my eyes, and I find them a healthy indulgence. But I know that this book brought upon Neil charges of 'sentimentality', making him defensive. He wrote to Professor Nakamura of his wish to portray a good man; of his risk, since 'Goodness runs closely parallel to sentiment'; of his concern lest 'sentiment' spill over into 'sentimentality'. On his behalf, I monitor my feelings.

The key to my feelings is found in another word: 'companionable'. Neil talked once on a beach in Portugal about those he called 'the few great companionable chaps' in literature. When I sent him a copy of Hesse's *Siddhartha*, he wrote back that he found it 'companionable . . . From the end of time, I can only say that that is what literature is for, the lit that matters.' *Young Art and Old Hector* is the most companionable of his books. In part it is so, because he himself was repeatedly in the company of these two characters about whom he felt most companionable, so much so that they lived on in his imagination into another tale. It is about companionship. It offers immediate access in its companionable kind of conversation. It is companionable in that each story dramatizes some familiar, universal piece of wisdom, some basic human paradox worth new contemplation. It is companionable because, as John Pick says, it conveys more fun in the reading and telling than any other of his books. In it, Neil seems to have discovered the fun of writing, and he never forgot it.

Its scale is companionable:

> It wasn't a very big loch. It was, indeed, quite a small one, but it had an importance of its own because the ground sloped upward all round it, so that when you stood near its edge you were in over the brink of a world shut off, with a new little world around you.

Its wisdom celebrates smallness, a value I have come to prize in a world of Great Expectations, Big Effects, Fat Pretensions. The book has much of its visual beauty in its evocation of relative scale. Hector revisits the green mound, the hill of faeries, after many years:

> In the fullness of his manhood . . . the place had seemed smaller than his childhood's memory of it, smaller and less important . . . But now the place did not seem small and unimportant. It was as big as it had ever been.

Part of Hector's wisdom is to help Art reduce in scale what seem terribly big problems to their true dimensions. Wisdom, we say, is getting things into proportion.

But here is one of its paradoxes. By virtue of smallness, the book becomes most universal. It must leave out much of the cultural particularity of bigger books. This one, however grounded in a local culture, is, like *Bloodhunt*, pared down to essentials, the basic polarities of folk motif and proverb, and thus has the universality of wisdom literature.

It is companionable because its essence is storytelling; it is not a novel. The storyteller and the novelist, Walter Benjamin suggests, are basically at odds. The novel arises from and appeals to the solitary individual. Story is traditional and communal, an affirmation of community; one tells stories to a companion. At this moment in his career — we see it happen to Finn in *The Silver Darlings* — Neil discovered that storytelling was essential to his art as well as to his vision of community. In earlier books, there is storytelling, but it is a theme, not a dominant mode. Now, it took on essential importance and kept it to the grand climax with the two essential human stories of *Bloodhunt*.

Not surprisingly, with the final stories of Art and Hector, Neil realizes the fundamental connection between storytelling and two of his essential, interconnected themes. The secret, a critic named Todorov suggests, is the essence of story, and in 'The Secret' Art learns how true that is. He is bursting with the secret of the illegal whisky-making he has seen, and this secret is his terrible new bond with Hector and others, the hallmark of community. The other side of secrecy is betrayal; note what I quoted to Dairmid from Simmel. If Art tells his secret, his story, he betrays Hector and may send him to prison. Keeping the secret is the absolute test of companionship, of community, as it is for old Sandy. The horror is that Art tells the other boy, the bully, and then beats him, has his blood on his hands. He tries to hide, cannot bear to see Hector, feels 'the terrible knowledge of betrayal deep in him'. He has committed the two worst of sins in Neil's communal code: betrayal and cruelty. But Hector and his allies have protected themselves, the gaugers are fooled, and, 'Old Hector, seeing far into Art's mind, withdrew the last sting of betrayal and left in its place the sweet balm that strengthens loyalty for the future.'

The book is precipitated into its final three stories. Art's great secret now is that his brother Donul will take him to the legendary river, but on the night, Donul suddenly goes away to work on a big cattle farm because there is 'nothing here' for him in these little places. 'The Little Red Cow', perhaps Neil's most perfect short story, simply portrays what happens to Donul and the little red cow, both from the small communal world of Hector, thrown into that big world where they cannot feel at home. Donul bravely tries. The cow is sold at discount to a butcher. 'From deep down in her the little red cow mooed.'

Donul's brave, reticent letter home mentions Art, and Art runs off to tell Hector the thrilling news. He tells his secret: Donul was going to take him to the river, and now he'll never see it. Casually, Hector says he'll take him, for it has 'come over' Hector that he would like to see it one more time himself. His last will be Art's first. It will be a handing on, not just of the river, but of the names of all the little places Hector alone knows. They talk. Will Art want to go off to the big world, too? Hector never did. Is he sorry? No, for if he had, he wouldn't be here with Art, wouldn't know all the little things here. That's a lot to know, says Art. ' "It's not the size of the knowing that matters, I think," said Old Hector, "it's the kind of the knowing." ' He will hand on all he knows to Art, and then Art will alone have the names, the secret, the story, and one day in a long time he will tell someone, too. 'If I thought you would do that,' says Hector, 'I would be happy.' 'Trust me,' says Art. 'I've trusted you often,' says Hector. There will be no betrayal between these companions.

And so, visiting the little places on the way, they walk together on their journey.

My hunch has been confirmed. It is different from *Bloodhunt*, yet essentially the same handing on. It is the book for the end of the day, and for the beginning, youth and age. The complexities, the dark obsessions, the ecstasies and creeds, all can come in the middle. You could read this first, Laura, if you were still young enough. Otherwise, wait and read it last, for somehow, in its handing on of what is essential, it is the only fitting farewell.

Rus

PS to Lorena: Loving thanks, as always, for giving me my own voice, and whatever sense of proportion I may have.

NEIL GUNN AND THE ETERNAL LANDSCAPE

NEIL GUNN AND THE ETERNAL LANDSCAPE

J. B. Pick

NEIL GUNN loved talk, metaphysical speculation, scientific theory, and all the patterns and arabesques which discussion can draw in the air, but he never strayed far from certain fundamental perceptions and beliefs, and unless these flights took off from experience and returned to experience he did not regard them as anything more than entertainment. Experience and the insights gained from experience were his touchstone for authenticity, and true conversation was for him a voyage of discovery with shared experience as a guide.

Over all the years I knew him he was fascinated by physics because physics was then the sharpest point of penetration into the nature of things; ironically, the more profoundly it probed the structure of the material world, creating theories and particles as it went, the more strangely matter seemed to behave, becoming at last a marvellous indeterminacy. The mystery remained for Gunn a continual source of interest and delight. Classical pattern and order would not have suited him at all. And yet the formulae of Euclid and Pythagoras were equally fascinating because of their very neatness and finality, their *quod erat demonstrandum*, which to him was like a poem, and a poem that worked.

If challenged to describe his mature attitude, I would put it like this: believe nothing until you have to; you have to when experience proves it to be true. In the meantime, remain alert to scientific discovery and the speculations which arise from it. Read books for the authentic insights they provide. If a book doesn't provide any, stop reading it. Explore the experience of people you meet. Everyone has a moment of illumination to offer.

Gunn was a courteous man who had developed over the years the ability to accept the unpleasant manifestations of others with apparent equanimity. His personal warmth and friendship, his pleasure in congenial company were legendary; he found his greatest enjoyment in the comradeship of shared ploys, and in conversation which undertook an intellectual or spiritual quest. But he always kept his reluctance to be 'touched'. Privacy had been since boyhood a part of his strategy for survival. He retained always a polite reserve in the face of intrusion, and if attacked in a crass and insensitive way would withdraw into icy detachment.

I don't think it is a contradiction that his novels are rich with intense feeling. Artistry demands that emotion is intuitively deployed for full effect, and what is controlled in life may be liberated in fiction. To reach literary maturity he had to move through adolescent turmoil and a period of personal bitterness painfully revealed in some early short stories and his novels *The Grey Coast* and *The Lost Glen*. He could recapture these emotions at need and they pulse through the inner conflicts of Finn in *The Silver Darlings* and some of the dark passages in *The Drinking Well*.

How did liberation come about? The boy Neil Gunn was one of nine children. *Morning Tide* and *Highland River* show him as a contributing member of a family with its own place in a working community. There were obligations which a boy might struggle to avoid, misunderstandings and quarrels with brothers, and complicated wrigglings and adjustments to establish a place in the hierarchy of age. But all Gunn's books show a particular need for escape into a loneliness which was not lonely, beyond the reach of even the friendliest eye. For Gunn it was essential to preserve an inner self to which no one must be allowed to penetrate and which no one must disturb. The social self could suffer discomfiture and assault without serious damage, provided that the 'inner self', which he felt to be separate and solitary, could be kept intact.

There is a revealing passage in the elusively autobiographical *The Atom of Delight* about the intrusions of school life.

At school one had to be wary, it was so easy to be *touched*. Even the most stolid could be dumb in a cunning way, but so long as there was no *knowing* assault on the inner citadel, rages and thrashings could be borne, like rites in some mysterious initiation which all had to go through on the way to adult freedom. Even irony and sarcasm, these *knowing* weapons, could be countered by a smouldering rage and hatred, which drew the inner circle toughly tight. The malicious pursuit, the persecution, had to be persistent before evasions like truancy took shape; and when truancy was impossible, the nerves at last took over, turning a boy's stomach against morning food, until the second self became vulnerable and 'lost' under the omnipresence of a fear more bewilderingly haunting than fear of the dark.

Characteristically, this is written as if it were generalization, but in fact it describes the author's own agonies. Even in recollection, wherever the 'personal' is involved, he seeks to avoid being 'touched', and the instinct is to defend, to draw the circle 'toughly tight'. In novels when the personal is disguised by embodiment in character and story, the most powerful and shaming emotions can be revealed without unease. It is as if the tale, not the author, is making the confession.

When he left the Highlands at the age of thirteen, first for Galloway, then London and Edinburgh, he was forced to see himself, the culture in which he was brought up, and all the traditions he had accepted as natural, through the eyes of alien beings who treated them as subjects for criticism and scorn. Story after story reveals his fear of returning home 'a failure', rejected and unable to establish himself in the world outside. Yet he referred everything that occurred 'outside' back to his inner self and his sense of the values of his own people, which he defended vigorously from any assault.

The real blow came when he returned at last to Caithness to find the fishing fleets of his boyhood gone, an atmosphere of malaise poisoning the air, and a general sense that new initiative was impossible, and decline permanent. He was deeply affected by this bitter disappointment. He identified his own inner distress with the depressed economic and spiritual condition of the Highlands. To ally himself with political efforts to change the situation he became an active nationalist; but the problem for an individual goes deeper than any political theory can reach (as many idealists discover to their cost). Human beings find it unendurable to exist without a sense of meaning and purpose, and this meaning and purpose to be satisfying must involve both communal and personal life. Writing was a way of asking 'How?' and 'Why?'

Gunn's struggle at this time can be expressed in literary terms as a fight to overcome the poetic melancholy and defeatism of Fiona Macleod (the pseudonym of William Sharp) and the ironic fatalism of Neil Munro. Fiona Macleod may seem comic to us now but to a young man growing up before the First World War this grey, sonorous, poetic sadness with its appeal to legend and the Celtic past was all that Highland literature had to offer at a time when new growth, clear vision, and active defiance were urgently needed – and it had an insidious attraction. Neil Munro, too, was the one major Highland novelist of the day, and his continual retreat into the acceptance of failure, his tendency to turn Stevensonian adventure into irony and withdrawal, was at the same time a red rag to a bull and an invitation to despair.

Because Gunn was so intensely sensitive in these matters – and ashamed of being susceptible – the initial rejection of *The Lost Glen* (the second novel he wrote), and its less than enthusiastic reception by the critics, went deep. The bitterness and hatred are so close to the surface in that uneasy book that they spill over into rhetorical excess and narrative melodrama.

No matter how many intellectual answers may be given to questions about Highland history, and to greater questions about human purpose, the intellect must operate together with the emotions if inner need is to be met. It was not until he returned in imagination to the recreation of boyhood, and wrote *Morning Tide*, that Gunn began to make the discoveries which enabled him to find a way through depression and bitterness.

Recollecting boyhood meant bringing back to consciousness not only moments of emotional turmoil and moments of communal warmth, but experiences which history and later travail could not touch, because they were strictly timeless. What is more, they brought the realization of an inner self which is not held in a circle 'toughly tight' against the outer world, but is alert, open and attentive to the life around it.

Gunn describes one such recollected moment in *The Atom of Delight* when the boy 'comes upon himself' while sitting on a rock in a stream. The self he comes upon is somehow a stranger of whom he feels a little shy. Who was aware of whom? And what constitutes the mood of contentment which he felt in wind and sun, with the 'lulling monotonous sounds' of the stream in his ears? Is a mood of contentment essential if such an experience is to occur? I suggest that all of us have such experiences, and manage to forget them, as if there were something in us which does not want us to remember; but if we try hard enough we can answer those questions ourselves. The boy was not then interested in questions of any kind, but simply conscious of a sense of freedom and release in a world of light.

By returning to childhood in *Morning Tide* Gunn recaptured the memory of such experiences — so important, so elusive and so unaccountably lost — and could then begin to explore his adult situation with the sense that he could cope with it and not go under.

There are times in his writing when I feel that he does not make the distinction between the inner self which has to be protected, and the 'second self' discovered by the boy in the stream. This is particularly the case in those novels where he has as protagonist someone I would call 'the Gunn character', with whom he tends to identify; this man must not be defeated or humiliated. But the deepest suffering involves humiliation, and if humiliation is not allowed by the storyteller, authenticity is endangered. Anything other than humiliation can be endured, but humiliation attacks the core of personality, and that is why the degradation of concentration camps destroyed its victims.

It is as if the 'second self' described in *The Atom of Delight* cannot of its nature assert its existence, but can only operate when allowed to do so by the will being asleep or occupied elsewhere. Discovery of the second self takes the whole personality by surprise, yet its function is limited to seeing, to being aware. This awareness is of more importance than any amount of 'doing', because deeds which are done without awareness have the opposite effect to the one intended. The second self alone is immune to humiliation, because it is fundamentally not individual at all.

The books in which Gunn brings this sense of awareness most vigorously alive are those in which the main character is not a 'Gunn character' at all, but someone entirely unlike the author with whom he can empathize with affectionate detachment, and who therefore embodies without strain the metaphysical themes he has in mind. I mean, for example, the beleaguered crofter Sandy in *Bloodhunt*, the archaeologist Grant in *The Silver Bough*, and Old Hector in *The Green Isle of the Great Deep*.

Drawing a magic circle to protect the individuality from psychic attack is as old as folk-belief, and was performed to make the symbolic actual. Gunn re-creates and adds to the content of this belief in a much-quoted passage from *Sun Circle*:

All that had been spawned out of night, of demon and black magic and gnashing horror, only in the end could they be kept at bay by one who after years of effort won thus within the circle of his own light. As the Sun put a circle round the earth and all that it contained, so a man by his vision put a circle round himself. At the centre of this circle his spirit sat, and at the centre of his spirit was a serenity for ever watchful. Sometimes the watchfulness gave an edged joy in holding at bay the demons and even the vengeful lesser gods, and sometimes it merged with the Sun's light into pure timeless joy.

That 'keeping at bay', that 'edged joy', is an expression of the self which the boy and the man strove to protect, to keep secret and intact, with which pride and individuality are identified. But the spirit within the circle in a 'serenity forever watchful', and capable of 'pure timeless joy' is that second self free from individuality in the sense that it sees without being concerned with the seer – indeed at the moment of seeing there is no seer, only awareness.

In the previous paragraph of the book it is said: 'The Master had often talked to him of glimpses . . . You did not understand truth: you saw it, and its clarity gave you an assurance that was profoundly happy, cool and transparent as a well, white as a bright noon, effortless as gulls' wings.' This is the experience of the boy in the stream, but deepened, intellectualized and transformed by adult recollection.

In the later novels Gunn tries to relate such inner realization to a perceived, elusive quality in the outside world. He describes this sense of a different reality experienced in moments of open awareness as 'the other landscape'. In perceiving it the outer and inner worlds reflect one another in such a way as to create a sense of unity. He describes his purpose specifically in a letter to his publisher, Geoffrey Faber, in relation to *The Well at the World's End*:

> May I, to begin with, give you a simple notion of what I have been trying to get at in the book? Where most novels of the more ambitious kind today deal with violence and materialism leading to negation and despair, I thought it might be a change if I got a character who would wander among his fellows looking for the positive aspects of life. Is it possible to pierce the negative husk, the dark cloud, even for a few moments, and come on the light, the bubbling well at the end of the fairy tale? Do folk still do it, ordinary people? Can this feeling be conveyed, the moment of wonder, of integration?

He is asking himself whether his own sense of the 'eternal landscape' can be expressed in such a way through incident and story as to arouse recognition in the reader. His books are filled with descriptions of the Highland landscape alive in its own secret intensity; this landscape had always for Gunn a dual quality of perfect familiarity and utter strangeness. Can he convey the sense that changes and gradations of light are inner as well as outer changes, and the two correspond at a level deeper than mood?

He writes in *The Other Landscape*: 'The prospect was a fair one, near and far, and the sea water, from the sun behind us, was a living blue; varied and austere, the wide sea was asleep and awake in its sleep.' Of course nature reveals something of which it is not conscious. In our normal 'closed' state we can't see it, and even when we wake up, and for a moment everything sparkles with meaning, we can't describe what we have seen. But the phrase 'asleep and awake in its sleep' is essential Gunn in that it reflects a feeling we have all had but can't bring back to consciousness so that in reading we realize it again.

If we look at the clear and simple account of the actual well in *The Well at the World's End*, and of the visit paid to it by Neil and Daisy Gunn, which reappears in the book as a visit of Peter Munro and his wife Fand, we may begin to grasp the symbolic force of what was a perfectly straightforward experience.

Peter Munro stared into the well that was so obviously dry . . .

His wife looked past his shoulder as if she could not always trust him to see what was before his nose, remarking thoughtfully, 'The old woman said there was water.' The pebbles on the well's bottom were blue and brown and beautifully clean, and it seemed to her that though the well had gone dry it still retained the memory of water, as pebbles in a cave the memory of the sea. It was shadowed by great clumps of fern and the bank was mottled with flakes of summer sunlight coming through the trees . . .

They return to the house and the old woman (as in a fairy tale) again assures them the well is never dry.

'Come here, Fand,' he said in the quiet voice that made her advance tentatively. 'Dip your kettle.'

'What is it?'

'Go on! Down with it.'

When the kettle touched the water she cried out as if she had been stung.

How beautiful, how incredible the waves of the crystal water! She got to her knees and watched them.

A few years ago Neil's nephew Dairmid gave me a sketch-map of the place where the well is to be found and I paid it a visit. Since Neil had told me the story that appears in *The Well at the World's End* in some detail, I knew exactly what to expect, and if the spot took some finding, that was just as it should be. But as always, reality and expectation don't match. The place was not the same now. A conifer wood had grown up since the 1950s, and the path was squeezed in between the crowding trees and a new fence. Indeed if I hadn't been told it was a path I wouldn't have known. Cut boughs lay everywhere and the ground was damp and slimy. Nobody had been along here for some time. I no longer expected to find a working well. What I did find, suddenly and by mistake, was a green cupboard set in a weedy bank. The cupboard had a lock but it was not secured. When I opened the cupboard, there was the well. But it was dry.

Neil had been right about the stones. They were beautifully clean and round and delicately coloured, as if collected and placed there with artistry by someone who loved stones. Since I can't resist them myself, I darted down a hand to take one from the bottom, a souvenir of the dry Well at the World's End. Light shivered everywhere in a flurry of ripples, and my hand leapt back as if from electric shock. I could not believe it, and crouched there for a long time, staring down at dancing water. It wasn't as if I hadn't been warned!

There is no need to make too much of this. Perfectly normal, everyone will agree. And yet I can't help feeling that there's something concealed in this mildly comic incident which I don't even want to put a finger on in case it obscures the stones. In one way the tale is simple, in another so unlikely as to be almost impossible. How could anyone be such an idiot! But then any approach to the Well at the World's End must be impossible. And when you get there the impossible is perfectly natural – or as natural as a dry well in a cupboard.

The well is just one of many instances of the ways in which Gunn tries to indicate the nature of the 'other landscape'. If I choose the other instances from lesser-known novels that is because to see the whole picture of Gunn you need to read all the books. He uses limited material again and again, but never writes the same book twice.

There are three types of approach: descriptions of experiences with a visionary, 'second-sight' quality; a rather self-conscious use of rhetoric to indicate 'otherness'; and the daily landscape and events described with such exact insight that they acquire an abnormal clarity. Here are three instances, one of each type, drawn from *The Silver Bough*. The archaeologist, Grant, is exploring a chambered cairn:

> There was an unusual stillness in the chambers, too; not that everything was without life, but that something had receded, leaving behind a sinister aspect . . . it was the presence of the annihilation after the act. It would not strike him; it would drain him through death to the negation of stone; and even then he would not be the stone, he would be the darkness.

This is the description of a feeling. There is nothing tangible there to discomfort Grant. We can make of it what we like. A delusion of Grant's would affect him equally; but I am sure we are not meant to interpret it as delusion. The occult, extra-sensory perception, invisible entities and so on occur only rarely in Gunn. When they do they are never pressed so hard that we could not see them as ambiguous. But they are always intended to be taken seriously. The episode of the haunted house in *The Well at the World's End* is a genuine incident which was told to him by one of those involved. The sensed presence of 'the wild man' in the cave after his death can be taken as a hallucination of a feverish Peter Munro, if the reader prefers it that way, but Peter himself is sure of its reality. Second sight, as in the book of that name, was familiar in tradition and local experience. Gunn had heard many accounts of it. Anyone who lives long enough in the Highlands will meet it, too. The appearance of the dead Annabel in *The Other Landscape* could be taken as a genuine apparition or as a telepathic phenomenon; but either way it is one of the most convincing incidents in the book, and the pivot of the story; if it is not authentic, the significance of the book is dissipated. Similarly, Finn's experience of a presence at the House of Peace in *The Silver Darlings* is crucial to his development. Gunn's inner rule would be that any such event had to establish itself in his mind as essential to the story and authentic in feeling; it would not be permissible to 'make it up'. That he held such incidents to be possible there is no doubt.

The too-deliberate rhetoric of 'otherness' which sometimes intrudes has about it a flavour of Fiona Macleod, and that atmosphere which he had set out to exorcize in order to become his own man many years before.

> The half-light, with its glimmer, had always had for him a curious historic reality, as though the world in this quiet hour turned itself into a stage whereon all that had been could once more be, but invisibly now, and therefore magically.

The feeling about evening light is authentic, but phrases like 'could once more be' and words like 'whereon' look back to Fiona, while 'stage' and 'magic' have a theatrical ring. If you are made to turn your eye away from the deepening twilight to the words themselves, the real magic is lost. How this real magic is obtained is given in *The Green Isle of the Great Deep*: 'You see, first of all you get the knowledge. Then you get the wisdom . . . Then . . . you get . . . the magic.' That is, you get the ability to realize the magic of what is actually there all the time.

It is in the simplest descriptions of the world in front of us, when only direct and straightforward words are used in their natural order, that the 'other landscape' comes alive:

> The light was growing green outside and fading away in the room. Things were settling down for the night, rocks and stones and the little pathway. The fowls were silent. The cat jumped up on the garden wall . . .

Nothing is hidden in this description. It is like well water, so clear it is invisible until the hand darts down to cause those ripples of light. But it is the Well at the World's End, which is a very simple place.

The same profound transparency occurs again and again in another novel which I rarely see mentioned: *The Shadow*. The girl, Nan, is recovering in the Highlands from nervous collapse resulting from experiences in wartime London. The breakdown was less the result of bombs and tension than of her fear and dread at the cold Marxist rigour in the minds of those around her. It drained her vitality. The first part of the book is Nan's own account of what she sees and feels as she explores the countryside in search of health. 'The yellow crocus was a tuning fork out of some sunny underworld, still holding the glow of the note.'

Poetry of this kind comes not from verbal skill but from insight. Nan's sensitivity to natural growth is a sign of her recovery. To feel the world breaking into spring is her way of building sanity and faith – and when the dark shadow of death and violence crosses her fields of light she suffers a shattering relapse. Final recovery becomes possible only when she finds a way to make the light internal.

'For what I want to do,' she writes, 'is to take you into that other world. It isn't, of course, another world, it's this world. But what has happened to our minds has also happened to our eyes, and we can't see it.' It is when 'this landscape' and 'the other landscape' are experienced as one that the light becomes internal. 'You are aware,' as Nan says, 'that everything has its own secret awakening.' And once she is continually aware of that, she becomes more than ever alive to the nature of what she is fighting against, of the threat to sanity and balance. 'We have murdered spontaneity . . . The faces of analysts, everywhere, with bits of matter on slides, and bits of mind on slides, saying: "That's all it is" . . . We have to rescue the intellect from the destroyers. They have turned it into death rays . . .'

Nan is afraid of those who 'think only', who analyze habitually, and so are unable to see. 'Seeing' in this sense is the insight which results from intellectual intuition as distinct from analytic reason; insight is perception freed from the distortions of will. Each experience of insight brings a sense of inner realization: 'Yes, that's *real*! I see it now.' What is realized can be a person, a crocus or a thought. It is this realization which gives life its vividness, reality and spiritual form, bringing with it wonder and delight. With each small awakening there is an actual growth of spiritual energy, of inner being. The book charts this growth in Nan's case without making it explicit, and does so through an account of immediate feelings and perceptions.

There is a saying of which Gunn became particularly fond at the end of his life in a very ancient Indian document: 'Look lovingly on some object. Do not go on to another object. Here, in the middle of this object – the blessing.' (*Zen Flesh, Zen Bones*, Penguin, London; 1971, p156.) He had practised that from an early age. Nan's quest is to find the blessing, and we read her account of 'looking lovingly on each object'.

Let me be explicit here that the word 'lovingly' means the exact opposite of 'sentimentally'. It means looking with a precise and affectionate attention so that the object is seen as it is and not as the observer has been accustomed to see it or would wish to see it or feels he is expected to see it, or so on.

There is only a single 'visionary' or 'extra-sensory' experience described in *The Shadow* and again this is left open-ended to be dismissed as imaginary (whatever that means) if the reader so wishes. It is based on an experience of Gunn's own.

Nan walks home with a strong sense of the approach of spring. 'It is an earthy fragrance, with a touch of burning wood or heather in it . . . No other scent *quickens* like this . . .' She has such a powerful feeling of being accompanied that she enters the house quietly to avoid meeting anyone. 'And then a queer thing happens – I don't close the door behind me. The impulse to leave it open is too strong . . . I mustn't shut out what has been accompanying me or following me. I mean the spring . . .' A kind of panic touches her and she escapes from the room 'just in time'.

> There was no imagined Figure of Spring. Male or female . . . It was the something in time before the Figure, in the way, say, that primitive folk first thought a mountain had a spirit. They did not in their minds give the spirit a human shape or really any other shape. I know this quite certainly. As it were, they did not dare! They might make something . . . as a *sign* of the spirit. But it wasn't the spirit itself, and certainly not its shape.

She goes on to explain the sense of lightness, freshness and grace in response to living things: 'You smile at the chaffinch as he skips upon the air. Everyone at some time has experienced this . . . You know it's true. *You know it's innate.* And you know we have conspired to murder it.'

Again and again Gunn tells his readers 'everyone at some time' has experienced this or that. The reader's response depends on whether he is willing to recall and admit to the experience. Gunn's intention, perhaps, is to make him search his memory. He also refers back frequently to the 'primitive' for the source of psychic perception, and when he says (as Nan says), 'I know this quite certainly,' he is serious. But this 'knowing' doesn't convince us unless we have recognized it ourselves. He is aware of this, and that we are entitled to ask, 'How do *you* know it?' His explanation would be that the 'knowing' is in the origin of the experience itself. We are the people who were at one time 'primitive' and in our basic psychological responses are primitive still. 'Knowing' is an intuitive opening to what is already there.

How do we 'know' it is there, and not an illusion we choose to accept? At the very heart of spiritual development are those moments when you 'know in yourself' something you formerly only guessed or thought or believed. There is nothing mysterious about this. At one time you may read something and it means little or nothing. Weeks or months or years later it comes back to mind, and you realize immediately what was intended: 'So that's what it meant!' The words are the same, but your consciousness has changed.

In the same way, at one time you see a flower and it is 'just a flower'. Then, under the influence of romantic feeling, it seems 'more than a flower', as if there were something concealed behind it. Finally you see it as it is, neither 'just a flower' nor 'more than a flower', but precisely a flower in all its vivid reality, and the being of a flower is for the first time alive to you in its own right. This is 'knowing in yourself'.

The effort to convey feelings and perceptions which are subtle and evasive and not only real but profoundly significant is characteristic of Gunn. People who react against this kind of thing and want every writer to be a hard-headed materialist won't appreciate the interior and external penetration of much of Gunn's writing, and will try to push or analyze it away. But it won't go. And it is just this tendency which is dealt with in *The Shadow*. To kill, condemn or despise emotion and the perceptions which combine feeling and intuition is to refuse insight its proper function and to close the mind to those discoveries which can change a man's life. People who thought that because of these subtleties Gunn was 'irrational' often received a sobering shock, for he was remarkably adept at logical debate.

In *The Green Isle of the Great Deep* Gunn devotes his attention to showing the effect of analytic reason applied without feeling to the administration of a state. The regime in the Green Isle uses analytic psychology as its tool, and a theoretical model as its guide. Gunn is clear about the effects of this: 'At the core of a theory or a plan, *in addition to the highest intention there can abide self-delusion and the last refinement of cruelty*'. To him cruelty is the unforgivable crime, and we get the feeling that in his eyes cruelty and the use of analysis are closely allied, because the analytic mind tends to see everything as a collection of parts rather than as a whole. Power, too, is itself a danger to balance and sanity, because 'they live in their heads, where the knowledge of power gives to a good intention the edge of a sword.' If you can do anything you want, why not go further and do everything?

To the administrators of the Green Isle order requires that there should be regulation, regulation requires the subordination of human oddity to a plan or a theory. The Fall can be seen – and has often been seen – as a Fall into disobedience. The logic of this is to see disobedience as 'evil', and man as inevitably disobedient, to be kept under control by a responsible élite. As it says in *The Green Isle*, obedience becomes 'the highest of all virtues' and the ideal becomes a society in which total obedience is the norm, the final aim being the creation of 'a corporate mind' which ensures that a whole people acts as one. Nazism and communism set out from different starting-points to achieve this end, destroyed millions, and failed. They failed because the need for freedom is innate, deep in the psychic stuff, and cannot be eliminated any more than hunger or the urge to reproduce. The original theology is wrong.

Gunn's theology in *The Green Isle* is one of love – a very practical concept indeed: 'For love is the creator; and cruelty is that which destroys. In between is the no-man's-land where men in their pride arrange clever things on the arid ground.' Gunn was convinced that this primacy of love, by which he meant a positive openness to the reality of others and to the world itself, was primordial. The relation of this idea to Christianity is considered in *Bloodhunt*. There is an ongoing disputation between the old crofter Sandy and the minister; the minister insists that there can be no order and morality without the discipline of the Church. But it is Sandy who says, in response to the minister's emphasis on the need for 'the fear of God', 'Either that or the love of Christ.' When, however, the minister prays, 'I bring you this new commandment: love one another,' Sandy reflects, 'We don't want to love one another. Words! Words! . . .'

At one point in *The Lost Chart* Gunn writes, 'Perhaps Christ was an archetype who would forever haunt the mind of man, with no chance of being destroyed; for when you destroyed him outside (as a projection) he merely returned, by an immutable psychological law, inside you.'

In a letter (to Gene Pick) about the references to Christianity in *Bloodhunt* he says, 'I suppose I must have been trying . . . to get a glimpse of that peculiar quality we have . . . called "goodness" . . . It seemed to me finally that it is not a specially Christian quality, not of any particular creed but, rather literally, primordial.' His belief was that without this 'primordial goodness' humanity could not have survived, and he tended to identify it with that instinct for co-operation within species which Kropotkin called 'mutual aid'.

The sense of human goodness did not make him blind to violence and evil. On the contrary, they are deep concerns in most of his books. The evil in the universe is the theme of his last novel, *The Other Landscape*, and the evil in man overshadows *The Lost Chart*. His writing from the beginning is the record of a personal struggle to overcome negative emotion and inner bitterness, and he was always willing to engage with the atmosphere of his time, however dark – but always in an attempt to discover the light through which to redeem it.

The Lost Chart is an uneasy, unsatisfactory novel written at one of the many crisis points in the Cold War. It conveys powerfully the atmosphere of obsessive concern with nuclear conflict and possible annihilation, with the growth everywhere of espionage and of the police state. Its theme is the sense of betrayal which taking sides in any complex human conflict always involves.

Our interest here is not in the novel itself so much as in the touchstones which Gunn provides for himself of what is permanent and worth defending. In this book, as nowhere else, he reveals private feelings about the culture of the Gael and his sense of his own heritage. Because of its isolation the island of Cladday has survived into the twentieth century with a living population and with its ancient culture intact. During the war the book's protagonist, Dermot, feels that his visit to the island with a naval vessel has affected the inhabitants as a betrayal, and now, in order, as he sees it, to defend the values of the island, he betrays it again. The sense of Cladday is given in a specific picture drawn directly from *Carmina Gadelica*, of old Anna curtseying to the new moon as she says, '*Many a one has crossed over the black river of death since you came here before*', and in descriptions of the island which simultaneously convey both outer and inner landscape:

> . . . the deep half-light of a summer night in the islands, in which everything from the black skerry to the edges of the sand dunes, from the grey face of the sea to the burning gold of the first stars, the breaking of a wave to the far away barking of a dog, or the near calling of a bird along the shore, was translated . . . And when it went beyond a certain translated beauty, into the grey silence when breath was not drawn, then it might not be experienced by anyone else, not like that.

I find this an odd passage. Does it mean that Dermot's sensitivity is so exceptional that no one else can share his perceptions? Or does it mean that every individual experiences such events differently? And phrases like 'translated beauty' and 'grey silence when breath was not drawn' take us close to the forbidden country of Fiona MacLeod which

Gunn had repudiated so strongly long before; they endanger the emotional privacy he was so keen to keep. In other books he had scrupulously avoided overt expression of emotion about Celtic culture, precisely because it would be identified with Fiona's sentimental melancholy.

Dermot is so deeply moved by Ellen's Gaelic singing that he forbids her to sing in his presence, and this ban is a covert way of asking her to break it. Whenever he describes her singing the shade of Fiona moves behind the words. 'It had silenced Ellen as it had destroyed the country . . . which he was always a little afraid of, because its beauty, its containing harmony, was sad with the mute cry of the forever lost.'

The point is made explicit when he writes, 'It was the quiet singing, the remembering within oneself, which Dermot found most difficult of all to bear . . . he knew the native reluctance to speak of such things, the instinctive secrecy with which they hid them from the stranger.' It is all the more extraordinary, then, that at one point Dermot (and Gunn) allow themselves to confess, without any effort to revise or tone down the extravagance of language, that a particular culture, threatened like all culture at the time with extinction by nuclear war, was personally precious and humanly meaningful at the deepest level.

The song – and the singing – had a whole civilization behind it, an attitude to life and death over a long time . . . It was the voice of Anna, the face of Anna, when she addressed the young moon, smiling across the black river and making her curtsey. The sea and the flowers on the machair; youth and the morning. Twilight. To you also I belonged once but I never can again for I am Youth. It was all there. It had manners. It was bright and sharp, and it grew mellow in age. It was sad to a depth that no lead sounded. Beautiful it was . . . Say it, say it once, say it was a beautiful thing that was murdered; even though they have made you feel a fool when you are saying it, say it. Say it once to your own heart, unashamed, before you grow strong again and ordinary again and deny it . . .

So much for the liberty offered by the novel! No one was more sensitive than Gunn to any charge of 'sentimentality' or 'escapism', and to lay himself open to both with the rhetoric of repeated phrases and reckless emotional commitment is an act of deliberate courage, because in my experience he was never unaware of what he was doing.

The other counter to the evil of betrayal and violence in *The Lost Chart* is in the devotion of Joe, the painter, to the necessity for inner and outer light. 'They do not understand,' says Joe, 'that you can only see a thing in terms of light,' and he tells Dermot that he wants to reach the power 'behind the light', accepting that 'it's behind the dark, too'. Dermot remarks that 'Joe had a habit of providing him with glimpses of another landscape.' These glimpses are essential if people are going to live through periods of darkness. 'The darkness creates drama ready-made for man; but man has to create his own drama of the light.' Evil, in other words, is easy, but 'primordial goodness' has continually to be rediscovered and reasserted; perhaps the purpose of man's pilgrimage is to create that drama of the light.

Gunn's references back to the Gaelic culture of *Carmina Gadelica*, and to his sense that his own people had a way of life which enabled community and individual to operate in harmony may be romantic or it may be realistic, but it is fundamental to his work.

The Well at the World's End is in a sense a farewell to this culture and this community which he has examined, re-created and celebrated for so long; but it is also a universal story based on the traditional notion of a legendary individual quest. Deeply embedded in it is the conviction that there is something fundamental which underlies both individual and community, reflected in the very landscape of the Highlands, which if seen with full awareness reveals 'the other landscape' too.

> The little fields, coloured with crops, the grazing cattle, a woman walking inside a wooden hoop carrying two buckets of water from a well, a man mending a roof, a boy rushing after a puppy dog, a trundling cart. Then he did a thing which he could never have conceived of doing before: he blessed that little community.

This is a picture not of the time when the book was written (the 1950s) but of his youth; trundling carts and buckets in hoops had disappeared.

A few pages later he remarks: 'By blessing the community, you bless yourself. Conversely, by destroying the community you destroy yourself.' And this is true.

Although the book tells us that Peter Munro, Professor of History, sets off on a holiday from his normal existence and even from his wife, he has a definite aim, to find out if ordinary people 'go through the boundary' into that state of being for which true vision becomes possible. But we start not with light but with danger, menace and doubt: a hazardous climb; an encounter with a man 'like one mysteriously there in a nightmare'; a night in a 'half-way house' between life and death; discovery of a sheep caught in a trap; a malicious joke played in a reputedly haunted house; a fight in the dark; and finally an escape from death only through a grotesque accident. Yet the air of the book is fresh and bright, the tone lively and humorous.

The question is specifically asked, 'whether evil does in fact exist,' and 'Actually I rather think I was moved by the notion that evil may exist – like many another force.' The answer given in the book – as the answer must be to all the great metaphysical questions – is ambiguous. At one point it is said, 'A feeling of evil beset him as he sat there. Dark streets and hanging yards. Evil was a horrible power that ran along a street and ran along a young arm to the fist. Evil was the black knife that struck.' At another point the malicious joke in the haunted house goes wrong, and the doctor who visits the scene concludes that 'an elemental force' has been let loose there. At another time, though, Peter is tormented and threatened by what he knows very well is a persecuting image born in his own mind.

There is a distinction to be made between, on the one hand, the 'evil' within men which grows because of individual failure to accept and follow personal insight, so that negative feelings are fostered, and balance and control eventually lost; and on the other hand, the idea of the force of evil acting on men from outside, to influence, pervert, and at last to destroy them.

I have to return to the fact that Gunn's touchstone for authenticity was always personal experience. He didn't write his novels as the result of reading moral philosophy. His own story of an encounter with a disintegrating force directed from outside is given both in *Off in a Boat* and *The Atom of Delight*. He describes this force as both 'pure evil' and more vividly as 'black electricity'. He was staying in the house of a friend and woke as the door of his room swung open. There was no one in the corridor. He then became aware of an attack directed on him from beyond the window, as if 'from the vaults of space'. In *Off in a Boat*, he says:

> It was not a being, a spirit, an imminent presence: it was a force; not a black magic but . . . a black electricity. It was quite impersonal, yet not a mere death ray; an emanation from an active principle of evil, as though the old conception of two principles in creation, good and evil, were in fact true, and the evil was at that moment having an undisturbed innings. The method of its operation was disintegration for its own sake, a disintegrating of the mind, the personality, and finally of the body.

In *The Atom of Delight* he adds that 'from somewhere far in space the rays were being directed at me, not so much by some controlling being or intelligence as by some intelligence in the source of the rays themselves.'

This is clear enough. But the matter is complicated in *The Other Landscape*, which deals with the fight against nihilistic aridity by a man who has lost his wife in appalling circumstances. Here the idea of two separate and opposing forces in the universe struggling for mastery is replaced by the idea of good and evil as being aspects of the same power, embodied in the aphorism, 'The Wrecker is God when He wrecks.' In this novel the character Menzies is saved from disintegration by his determination to find the true nature of the eternal landscape beyond the realm of the Wrecker. He achieves it only as the result of a vision of his dead wife Annabel. Since Annabel is seen clearly by the narrator too, we must take it that in some sense she is really 'there'.

Throughout the book there is a close implied relationship between the creative process (personal and universal) and the love between human beings; and there is the profoundly interesting idea of 'guilt that is at the heart of Creation itself, the Wrecker's guilt'. This would give us a theology of conflict within God being worked out in time so that every decision by each individual contributes to the result – a definition of freedom in terms of responsibility. And it is said, 'Against that darkness, man has the light, the warmth, the other insight which love has fashioned for him as his sole weapon on the eternal quest.' The love Menzies shared with his wife Annabel remains undeniably real in experience even after her death, and his rescue comes from his living awareness of her gift of light. May I say here that if this were merely an abstract idea or an expression of romantic hope Gunn might legitimately be accused of sentimentality, but it is not. It is a statement of his own realization of the nature of the love between himself and his wife Daisy.

There is one thing to add to this. In *The Lost Chart* Gunn quotes several times the prayer for seafarers in *Carmina Gadelica*:

> Thy hand upon the tiller,
> And Thy love behind the wave.

His projected title for the book was *Behind the Wave*.

The 'something' which is beyond the Wrecker cannot be discovered in the realm of thought, but only by direct perception, when insight operates without the interference of the will. This sort of discussion is very difficult, and rather than get carried away into abstractions I will end with some consideration of the poetic flashes in *The Green Isle of the Great Deep*, which to my mind is the book of Gunn's in which his intellectual intuition is working with the most spontaneous clarity and at the highest creative pressure, so that there is no gap at all between perception and the language which expresses it, and we are moved by the sheer force of insight into a knowledge we didn't know we had. This is evidence of the capacity which poetry has to 'break open mind' and to bring about realizations which stay with us although we can't define them.

What are we to make, for example, of passages like this?

> It was a big tree and wide-branching, and the apples that grew on it were ruddy and gold in the evening light. The more Old Hector looked, the quieter the tree became, until its stillness held the beauty that being pure was strangely ominous, and into his mind came the words: *The tree of knowledge of good and evil.*

Why should pure beauty be 'ominous'? Purity can either be 'empty' – a lack of impurities – or 'full' – everything held within the mind in a state of fruitful harmony. Its fullness might then be 'ominous' with simultaneous threat and promise, like the universe itself.

And what of these passages?

But all the words were like birds in the air, excited birds that could not land. When Robert stood still, however, all the cries died away, and the words came to rest on him as on a dark tree. The upward gleam of his eyes gave space to the tree and invisible branches.

Or, 'The night itself heard, and shivered like broken glass in all the far windows of space.'

Poetry can unite incompatibles and liberate unrealized possibilities so that surprising marriages take place between feeling and reason. We sense Robert in that description experiencing extra dimensions and fulfilling potentialities he did not know he had. He has realized the true depth of nature of his wife Mary, and her capacity for action, understanding and sacrifice. It changes his view of the world. But this is not said. What is said is indefinable.

And when 'the night itself heard' we know that we are in the region of events which go beyond normal reality; God is about to enter the story. And when He does, it is to the boy Art in the guise of a friendly old man he thinks he has met before, while Hector sees '. . . the bearded face of the man who awaited him seemed . . . to be the face of someone he had seen long ago in a tall mirror at the end of a landing in a forgotten house.'

There is a dream-resonance here, as if dream and waking were working together to produce a power for which there is no obvious source, lights shining without a generator. What is happening, then? Is this imaginary house of Hector's haunted? The house of the mind is haunted by God, the Devil, and all sorts of spirits and forgotten archetypes which come without being bidden, and were there when men lived in caves, and will still be there when they live in plastic bubbles on the surface of the moon. If we get too far separated from the ancient movers in the mist, we will end up lost and wandering in a desert of empty skyscrapers.

The figure of the man Hector saw was disconcerting because he so closely resembled Hector himself – and Hector is not accustomed to looking in mirrors – but it resembles also some image of the old man of the tribe, as seen by a certain people at a certain time: specifically, the Highlands of Scotland when Hector himself was a boy. God comes to each people as the figure which has gathered most depth and power, whether prophet, man-monster, White Goddess, overwhelming idea, or bearded sage. And yet He evades finally all knowledge, speculation and wisdom. The water in the well at the world's end is so transparent that the coloured stones at the bottom can be seen in all their simplicity.

It is said that for Sandy in *Bloodhunt*:

> The country of the spirit had been gradually taking shape, gathering a feature here, a snapshot there, a certain light, a vague climate; but mostly when he wanted to catch a whole glimpse of it and enter its mood, he saw only the hills, the lochs, the bracken, the birches, the long tongue of water lilies where the trout fed and set their circles on the still water . . .

The country of the spirit is the country of the eyes and the mind; it takes shape as the eye sees more and the mind understands more. For Gunn you arrive 'elsewhere' when you are most alertly *here*; but for this there is a necessary prerequisite. As it says in *The Well at the World's End*, 'All he had to do was to forget himself. Immediately the ego with its demands was forgotten, everything was alive naturally in its own place . . .' But to forget yourself is the most difficult thing in the world to do.

'In the region of shadows,' Gunn wrote, 'you have to make contact, if you can, with what you realize does not change.' What is it that does not change? The faculty in us which is capable of seeing what is actually so, and which has nothing to do with the ego at all. This faculty is there from the beginning, but to operate correctly must be developed by following insights step by step and stage by stage towards a final completion which will never be reached.

MYTHIC REGENERATION OF SCOTLAND

NEIL GUNN AND THE MYTHIC REGENERATION OF SCOTLAND: THE TWO GREAT EPIC CYCLES

Douglas Gifford

SINCE THE Act of Union binding Scotland to England in 1707 and the aftermath of the Jacobite rebellions, Lowland Scotland and the Highlands have existed in a state of cultural division. Despite the achievements of the Scottish Enlightenment of the eighteenth century in philosophy, history, and in the sciences outstandingly, and despite the astonishing contributions of Scotland in the nineteenth century to the process of Western industrialization and British imperialism, most Scots – and perhaps all Highlanders – have a sense of unease concerning their own and their country's final identity. This unease must also be understood within the context of a national culture striving to rediscover a sense of historical purpose and to shake off the defeats inflicted from within and without. These defeats involved loss of political self-determination, loss of regional identities (such as in the Highlands after 1746 and the Clearances), and devastating industrial change to an essentially rural Scotland. Perhaps most destructive of all was the *anomie* of the nineteenth century, that fatalistic feeling of the pointlessness of defying social and cultural change imposed by the vast and impersonal forces far beyond local community control.

It is in this grand Scottish context that we must now view the achievement of Neil Gunn; more than any other writer it seems to me that he, in the trilogy of *Sun Circle* (1933), *Butcher's Broom* (1934) and *The Silver Darlings* (1941), followed by the epic duality *Young Art* and *Old Hector* (1942) and *The Green Isle of the Great Deep* (1944), plumbed the depths of Highland and Lowland Scottish self-doubt and historical agony, yet triumphantly emerged with a mythic refashioning of identity, with an affirmative statement that the Highlands and Lowlands of Scotland could turn tragedy to positive recovery. The achievement is Tolstoyan, amounting to perhaps the greatest, most affirmative, and most artistically effective and coherent contribution to Scottish literature and to Neil Gunn's country, on a par with MacDiarmid's *A Drunk Man Looks at the Thistle* (1926).

Since 1707 Scottish writers were faced with a basic choice: either they moved their sensibility outwards, repudiating or transcending (depending on one's point of view) their locality, their Scottish dialect, and their sense of Scottish identity, like so many of the sophisticated writers of Enlightenment Edinburgh such as John Home, Henry Mackenzie, or Hugh Blair, and Anglo-Scottish regional writers such as Boswell and Carlyle, or they asserted (with attendant personal unsureness and constant doubt as to whether to use English or Scots) a broadly defiant and prickly Scottishness. This resentment came out in the work of Allan Ramsay and Robert Fergusson in their complaints about the fashionable Italianizing or Anglicization of native Scottish song and verse, and in their occasional, but ambitious, attempts to elevate their local Edinburgh cameos and ironic sketches into a poetry which could see beyond the local to the Scottish national, and to an awareness of Scotland in time and in tradition. Stumblingly Ramsay tried this throughout his very mixed work. Two ambitious long poems, 'Wealth or the Woody' (gallows) and 'The Vision' were particularly successful in this attempt to speak for a whole Scotland. The first pours scorn on English folly in the South Sea Bubble scandal of 1720, looking (in Scots), with a rare confidence in Scottish mercantile canniness, at speculation madness in Britain; the second, through the pretence of being the work of a medieval Scottish poet, 'A.R. Scott' (Allan Ramsay, Scotsman) purported to talk of the Wars of Independence of Wallace and Bruce, but masterfully and cunningly made stark and vivid commentary on Scotland's despair then applicable to the country's woes of the present in the post-Union period, prophesying that Scotland would turn in resurgence against its English oppressors – as had happened in 1715.

But it is not the detail of such holistic national poetry that interests us here so much as the creation of the type: it is the beginning of a kind of visionary poetry of national regeneration through satirical perception of faults internal and external. Fergusson moved towards it in 'Auld Reekie' (1773), where the overall shape of his account of Edinburgh at work and play over a weekend began to take on archetypal overtones; the events and people portrayed became emblematic, even heraldic, and the perspective on them moved back to view Edinburgh in a setting of history, and, spatially, in the context of the Forth and Fife. And even more, in 'The Ghaists', Fergusson detached himself from immediacy; here, in an enchanted night in Greyfriars graveyard, the ghosts of two liberal and heroic Scotsmen, George Heriot and George Watson, philanthropists and founders of schools for impoverished Scots children, arose from their graves, awakened by English injustice. Fergusson used them as archetypes for an older Scottish humanism and identity. And while Burns had poetry in the genre, his 'The Vision' (1762) failed to follow through to any significant comment on Scotland's destiny. Burns was much more successful when rooting his most ambitious poems on Scottish character and peasant resilience in local matters, such as the wonderful portrayal of the triumph of humanity over bigoted religion in 'The Holy Fair', or that fable of the essential folk, 'The Jolly Beggars'. And has not Tam O'Shanter become the quintessential symbol of the ordinary Scotsman who has to face grim reality, just as 'Holy Willie's Prayer' stands for the arrogance of the worst aspects of the Scottish Church?

And in realizing the emergence of this epic and national poetry of whole Scottish identification, we are indebted to William Donaldson, who has in recent works revealed to us that beyond the literary canon another Scotland was speaking wholly for itself. His *The Jacobite Song* (1988) demonstrated the continuity of popular Scottish culture after the Union and found living nationalism expressing itself through the rediscovery of popular song and political satire, throughout the eighteenth and into the nineteenth century. This great surge of national consciousness was to underpin the rise of the novel of mythic regeneration in the nineteenth century. For it does seem that poetry retreated from the role of carrier of national consciousness from Scott onward – perhaps because Scott so firmly relegated the matter of

Scotland to the past in his poetry, if not in his fiction. Certainly Hogg's 'visionary' poems like 'Kilmeny', or even the ambitious *The Queen's Wake* (1813), remove insight into Scottish identity into the realms of fairyland and quasi-Christian mysticism, while William Tennant's undoubted poetic genius at the same time preferred to turn the 'matter of Scotland' to burlesque farce, in *Anster Fair* (1814) and *Papistry Stormed* (1827). There were, as Donaldson emphasizes, later nineteenth-century self-taught poets (like William Thom and Janet Hamilton) – but such were the problems of poverty and the lack of intellectual support for them that their work, while often outstanding, is perforce limited to powerful attack on immediate problems of social and sexual injustice, rather than identifying with a Scotland which had so betrayed their dialect, their livelihood and their self-respect.

In all this we look forward to Gunn's culminating place as a maker of Scottish regenerative myth; but he cannot be seen in true perspective unless we can understand the immensity of the task he undertook. After poetry's comparative failure, only the novel attempted to diagnose Scottish ills. It did so obliquely. Apart from Galt, George Macdonald and Douglas Brown, and in the popular press attempts too often marred by melodrama, most nineteenth- and early twentieth-century writers of achievement preferred to escape to historical or rural Scotland. We should not miss their genuine insight into the divided loyalties and troubled psyche of Scottish culture, however, recurrent themes of morbid and fragmented self, in divided family and nation, show Scott, Hogg, Galt, Ferrier, Oliphant, Macdonald, Stevenson, Alexander, Brown, and MacDougall Hay (to list the major novelists) to be well aware of the tensions threatening Scottish society and identity. Broadly, they worked on two fronts: satirically demonstrating Scotland's unhappy post-Union disease, its prevailing commercial greed and 'Mrs Grundy in Scotland' (Willa Muir's phrase for Victorian piety of a quality more snobbish and hypocritical than real); and – but all too rarely and unsuccessfully – trying to create an affirmative model by way of epic fiction which would show a Scottish hero or heroine transforming their own and their community's life in a way which could stand as an example to the fragmented Scotland of industrial nightmare and lost community.

That is simply to say that the best of Scottish tradition in fiction, of the century before Gunn, saw Scotland either negatively or positively.

Negatively, Scott identified all the civil wars (outstandingly those of religion and Jacobitism) which have torn Scotland, together with the loss of political will and social justice which he laments in *The Heart of Midlothian*; Galt satirized small-town chicanery and big-town Mammon-worship in *The Provost* (1822) and *The Entail* (1823); Hogg identified the roots of religious bigotry in *The Justified Sinner* (1824); Ferrier attacked the new Edinburgh and Scottish class pretentiousness in *Marriage* (1818); while Mrs Oliphant, Macdonald, Alexander, Stevenson, Brown and Hay all saw corrosive materialism destroying traditional community and social charity.

But it is the positive tradition which culminates in Gunn. And once again Scott inaugurated this, with his trilogy of novels seeking to forgive the betrayals of the past: *Waverley, Old Mortality, The Heart of Midlothian*. Each worked within a pattern of a divided Scotland, torn between past and present, between outlaw disorder, and establishment and excessive authority, the cause and values of an older Scotland repressed and attacked by the newer, Anglicized and economically prudent Scotland. Each showed Scott trying, with his profound (and new) sense of the way history works, to reconcile the internecine forces. Each tried to find a way of telling Scotland's story which would heal old wounds, allowing destructive legend and memory to become distanced, so that what had been in time past mortally offensive was pushed into myth and became an 'old mortality' – the literal meaning of that novel's title. But Waverley – the young protagonist of Scott's first novel – failed, because he could not take the strain of a national and bridging role, the novel being more of a study in delusive romanticism, in which Waverley was caught up in a cause he did not understand and in which he had no genuine role, being English. In *Old Mortality* Henry Morton was much more credible: son of a Presbyterian leader, university educated, tolerant and sensitive, he stood for the suffering conscience of Scotland, caught in the middle of religious civil war. But he was more. He began to transcend his passive plight, becoming the active mediator, trying to bring reconciliation and fair compromise to the troubled ranks of his own side, as well as between Presbyterians and Episcopalians. The comparative failure of this great novel was not Scott's so much as Scotland's. It was history itself which defeated Henry Morton's role as Scottish healer, since it was historical events, rather than Morton's choices, which forced his exile to Holland. Scotland's gaining of established Presbyterianism was not due to him, but to the fact that William of Orange endorsed it, as it were, by the way. These decisions were not taken within Scotland by Scots, but without, by foreigners.

Scott therefore turned to a new kind of Scottish protagonist, and one who would have the most profound effect on the later Scottish novel, and on Grassic Gibbon and Gunn particularly. In choosing a 'cowfeeder's daughter' as his new heroine, in *The Heart of Midlothian*, Scott deliberately moved away from conventional figures of fiction. He also moved away from 'history', instead now setting Jeanie Deans's story in the context of a fairly minor Edinburgh riot after the Act of Union. Since the events of Scottish history did not permit of a grand historical hero – not even the Duke of Argyll! – Scott turned to find Scottish regeneration elsewhere, in the timeless resilience of the Scottish folk themselves rather than great leaders, just as Hogg, Galt, Macdonald, Oliphant and Stevenson would do after him, and just as the Scottish Renaissance later emphasized in fiction and poetry. More clearly than anywhere else in his work, Scott showed here sick Scotland, summed up in the symbol of the rotten Heart of Midlothian, the execrable gaol of Edinburgh, the barbaric Tolbooth in the High Street. And it stood as symbol of the rotten hearts of so many around it: Captain Porteous, whose barbarity started the riots which bear his name; the sick magistracy and lawyers who hunted down Jeanie's wayward but pitiable sister for her concealed pregnancy; the local mob, so fickle and hard-hearted. This disease, this Scottish rottenness, argued Scott, was partly due to loss of identity ('Naebody's nails can reach the length o' Lunnon,' says a High Street harpy), and the riots are as much due to Scottish resentment of this as anything. Justice – from Westminster and the decadent court of George I – has gone sour, and Scotland yet sourer, in its vicious treatment of pardonable offenders, folk-heroes like the traditional smuggler, Wilson. Set against this sick heart is Jeanie, the genuine heart of Scotland ('Midlothian' here, placing her in the middle of the country). Her walk to London is a quest for justice *and* a model of grass-roots, peasant-based initiative and integrity. Her fulfilment is her benign rule in her domain at Roseneath, given to her and her minister by the Duke of Argyll. There she continues to perform her 'magic', her wonderful feat of converting enemies and regenerating

Standing stone, Dunbeath (Glyn Satterley)

Sheep, sea and shoreline near Dunbeath (Glyn Satterley)

Crofter, sheepdog and sheep near Dunbeath (Glyn Satterley)

Dunbeath Harbour (National Library of Scotland)

Larachan, Inverness (Dairmid Gunn)

Braefarm House near Dingwall (Dairmid Gunn)

Kincraig overlooking the Cromarty Firth (Dairmid Gunn)

Kerrow near Cannich (Dairmid Gunn)

Dalcraig on the Black Isle (Dairmid Gunn)

Shoreline and sands at Dornoch (Glyn Satterley)

North Caithness towards Castletown (Glyn Satterley)

T. S. Eliot relaxing on a visit of Faber directors to Inverness, 1938
(National Library of Scotland)

Neil Gunn and Maurice Walsh at Tobermory, 1937
(National Library of Scotland)

Sir Alexander MacEwen and Neil Gunn with three German visitors, 1936
(Malcolm MacEwen)

Part of a ceilidh scene from the film The Silver Darlings:
two old crofters dance to the pipes (National Library of Scotland)

Neil Gunn the angler (National Library of Scotland)

Neil Gunn in reflective mood (Dairmid Gunn)

Neil Gunn sitting in his favourite armchair (National Library of Scotland)

the fallen. Roseneath is an island in the novel, if not in fact; and Scott meant it to be a microcosm of Scotland, with its mixture of warring Highland and Lowland elements brought into harmony through Jeanie's essential peasant goodness.

We do not have space to follow Scottish fiction's development of this model here. Suffice it to sum up the main line of descent to Gunn: in Hogg's exemplary Borderers in *The Brownie of Bodsbeck* (1817), or *The Three Perils of Man* (1822); or Galt's regenerative minister in *Annals of the Parish* (1821), emphasizing community and charity; George Macdonald's epic pair of novels in *Malcolm* (1875) and *The Marquis of Lossie* (1877), where the humbly born Malcolm becomes the marquis, yet insists on keeping his native tongue and community values, so that Macdonald's final statement is politically and culturally radical in its repudiation of class and establishment privilege; Mrs Oliphant's *Kirsteen* (1890), where her young protagonist goes on her quest, from Argyllshire to London, to find a less repressive society and an expression for her native shrewdness and independence; William Alexander's unpretentious, powerful picture of *Johnnie Gibb of Gushetneuk* (1871), the simple crofter who acts as a regenerative model for his community far more effectively than the more conventional leaders of big house, church or school.

It is a measure of the loss of confidence of Scots in the society that had changed so radically from rural to urban that later Victorian and Edwardian fiction was generally negative. Stevenson's divided family with its polarized brothers in *The Master of Ballantrae* (1889), brothers destined to share the same grave, sums up the disillusioned feeling that Scotland was – if looked at seriously, rather than through the distorting lens of the Kailyard novels, those falsifications of rural life which flourished at the end of the century – a dark country. David Balfour of *Kidnapped* (1886) and *Catriona* (1893), Stevenson's most politically conscious protagonist, decided after witnessing Scottish political betrayal and counter-betrayal to have nothing at all to do with public affairs in Scotland, while his great unfinished work, *Weir of Hermiston* (1896), was quite simply anachronistic and perhaps unfinishable.

Into this pessimistic literary world came Gunn. He was clearly aware of the fatalism of the 'Celtic twilight' of Fiona Macleod in the 1890s, the negative realism of *The House with the Green Shutters*

(1901), and its Highland equivalent, MacDougall Hay's *Gillespie* (1914), with their pictures of social disintegration through greed, and the loss of the younger generation which should have followed. The theme of the failed student who comes back home in disgrace, embittered and alienated from his own community, was to become one of the most insistent in Gunn's work. His first novels, *The Grey Coast* (1926) and *The Lost Glen* (1929), are profoundly concerned with the state of Scotland and the north-east. Here is not the place to tell in detail of Gunn's post-war depression concerning the end of the herring industry as it had gloriously been in the nineteenth century, the failure of the Great War to offer hope to the Highlands, or the even older sense of profound apathy dominating not just the north, with its aftermath of government antagonism towards clans in the wake of the Jacobite rebellions and all the subsequent misery of the Clearances, but also the Lowlands, caught in the depression and the backwash of the English economy. Hart and Pick have given us in their great biography, *Neil M. Gunn: A Highland Life* (1981), a sensitive and perceptive description of the young exciseman's bitterness and anger about his country's neglect and stagnation, economically and culturally, as does Pick's illuminating *Selected Letters* (1987) and A.G. McCleery's collection of Gunn's political and cultural essays, *Landscape and Light* (1989), complements them with Gunn's actual thoughts on Scottish disintegration and the need for regeneration. We are concerned here with the sheer magnitude of literary achievement in the two epic cycles in which Gunn deals with the state of Scotland and the north. But let us first lay to rest two hoary and unworthy accusations concerning Gunn's achievement.

First, Gunn was not concerned to assert Highland spiritual supremacy. He is at pains to emphasize in his essays and autobiography that he knows his luck in having spent his early years in a 'good' community. There are plenty of places in the Highlands and Islands *not* like this, he knows, where Clearance and religious pressure (to name only two negative forces) have spoiled traditional community. In *The Silver Darlings*, chapter 8, 'The Spirit and the Flesh', exemplifies such a place, and shows Finn, Gunn's protagonist, realizing what social distortion could, and did, take place. *The Lost Glen* and *The Grey Coast* show the dispiriting bleakness which lack of personal and community identity can bring; such spoiling leads in these novels to emigration and murder, hardly endings compatible with 'spiritual superiority'. Second, and linked to this is the apparently limiting description of Gunn as 'novelist of the north'. Yes, he is, in the sense that he sets his novels there; but no, he is not, if what is implied is that local character and theme is all his aim and effect. If Gibbon or Scott or Galt can be allowed to speak for Scotland generally via villages in the Mearns, Edinburgh peasants, and Ayrshire ministers, then surely we must allow the possibility of the Scottish – and universal – statement emerging from Gunn's similarly archetypal protagonists and situations?

Morning Tide (1931) is Gunn's shift to affirmation. In the boy Hugh, Gunn found the perspective of newness which refashions tragedy into comedy, defeat into challenge. We sense Gunn's steadying, here; he has touched the bottom of his despair. Simultaneously he was working politically in Inverness, helping forge a unified Scottish National Party which, he hoped, would turn around the fatalistic apathy of centuries. As a civil servant he accepted he could not be the overt politician, but had to be instead the reflective and creative thinker and artist. (That is not to deny his very practical activities in politics and on various public bodies concerned with issues like fisheries, hydro-electricity and hospitals.) What he now undertakes is nothing less than a fundamental enquiry into the roots of Scottish folk and community history, with two broad aims; first, to find where Scottish community had lost its innocence, egalitarianism, identity and promise; and then to relocate the source, as a source of endurance and abiding worth, so that by finding essential qualities these can be made to conquer the betrayals and fatalism which have become the settled, bleak rhythms of centuries-old despair.

Sun Circle has been greatly misunderstood. Its apparent shapelessness and opacity of ideas have concealed from too many readers its subtlety of purpose and rich complexity of folk-theme. Like Goldings's *The Inheritors* (1955), it tries for that most difficult of communications, whereby the vastly different conceptualization of what is virtually the prehistoric mind makes itself known to us. Naomi Mitchison has tried it more recently and less successfully in *Early in Orcadia* (1987), to my mind overtrivializing and reducing her first men and women of Orkney, where Gunn allows an overwhelming richness and immediacy of smell, animal awareness, weather, light and dark –

all presented from an authorial attitude deliberately timeless and unidentified, so that from the very opening we don't know whose is the 'long gaze' which moves from Orcades to Western Isles, to narrow on Iona. This is a view of Scotland entire, sweeping over forest and valleys and mountains like some airborne over-mind or collective unconscious, drawing the reader back through time and contemplation of prehistoric Scotland to land in Gunn's own Dunbeath, under the sea-cliffs, and wandering inland to an unnamed valley, to a woman and child. This is the beginning of Scotland's history and Gunn's quest.

To impose order on this deliberately wandering, sensual, primitive, yet sophisticated novel is artificial. It must be attempted, however, to show how the quest moves on. We are back with the Raven tribe in the eighth century – an ancient people, Picto-Celtic, whose ruling place, the tower of Drust, the chief, has been in the same place since time out of mind. Darkness surrounds its origins, and darkness here is seen (as by MacDiarmid) as a creative, natural element, in Manichean opposition to the light. The image of sun circle here stands for a circle of life, of ritual and song, against the dark, or in intuitive balance with it. 'In my locality . . . there did exist traces of the ancient kindness and interest of the Simple Folk. It goes far beyond the Gaelic . . .' wrote Gunn to Gibbon in 1935, reminding us that from the outset he thought of his roots as representing a Scotland far beyond the confines of an ideological Gaidhealtachd, and that in this first part of his quest he was imaginatively re-creating his vision of what the norm of living had been for this simple people for thousands of years. In *Whisky in Scotland* (1935) he ties Gaelic tradition to a Pictish base like that of his 'sun circle': 'the old Gaelic poetry was sun-bred, exuberant and yet vigorous, charged with life or the wild singing of death, positive . . . There was a flame at its core. Slowly the flame died down . . .'

A patterning of the opposition between darkness and light substantially replaces conventional narrative in this unusual and experimental novel. The dark girl Breeta contrasts with the golden daughter of the chief, Nessa; Aniel, the disciple of the Druid Master, is similarly set against Viking Haakon, leader of the raiders (who are one part of the destruction of the sun circle of the community of the Ravens). Gunn constantly arranges subtle pairings. The Druid Gilbrude and the Grove are set against the Columban missionary

Molrua and his house of Christian peace downriver; ancient darkness against new light. The notion of sacrifice itself provides a central contrast. Gunn avoids judgment, simply showing an ancient ritual of propitiation in which enemies are burned, virgins given to the knife, or animals offered up, as one way of coping with the darkness, as opposed to Christian self-sacrifice, as when Molrua allows himself to be butchered by the Vikings. Neither is better, although the Christian way may be the ritual of the future, as the Druid Master allows. Judgment is suspended likewise in the matter of gods. Gunn suggests that the old gods – Leu, the sun god, the Dark Ones, Rhoss, the moor-spirit, together with serpent and bull spirits, had a potency as valid as Christ's. The unusual authorial perspective allows – as always with Gunn – that such presences, pagan or Christian, emanate from the essential myth-making part of the human mind, and are thus to be treated with equal consideration. Ritual likewise has its place as deeply necessary spiritual metaphor expressed in action. Here, walking sunwise in a circle around a dwelling, or the symbolic dowsing and relighting of fires symbolizing regeneration is set against the new Christian practices of Molrua and his main convert, the chief's wife Silis.

The timeless authorial perspective, acting almost as the detached spirit of the race, may allow all such oppositions and tensions as equally valid; the immediate considerations of the Ravens, caught between the demands of Christian submission and meekness, and the need for vigorous aggression against the invaders, do not. All the antagonisms latent between active paganism and passive Christianity are focused in the sensitively presented, awkward tension between Drust and Silis. Drust has to hold to the old and potent dark ways, since only thus can he find his *mana*, his almost magical power, to lead as true chief. Silis, the archetypal civilizing force, cannot understand the desperate nature of the Viking threat – although it has to be said that Aniel's father, the bard Taran, suggests a middle course of temporary withdrawal which implies that both chief and wife are wrong. (The failure of this flicker of leadership from within the tribe itself, unusual and ignored, will later be seen as epitomizing the characteristic failure of the Celts and the Scots, a lack of confidence in self or group when devoid of leadership.)

Fatally flawed from within by the loss of that 'sun-bred . . . wild singing of death, positive and challenging', Drust and the Ravens are slaughtered. Silis, in tragic recognition of her misperception, kills herself. As with *Butcher's Broom* and *The Silver Darlings* and *The Green Isle*, we are given a glimpse of early harmony or hope, only to have it broken, as the promise of so much Scottish history itself has been repeatedly broken. Gunn's method is the same in all these novels. From tragedy and disruption, from the breaking of the circle, the shattered survivors have to regenerate themselves. And here the novel reveals its true complexity. Gunn is offering no easy answers to the problem of regeneration, but rather suggesting a need for simultaneous retreat (to dark sources of instinctive power) and progression (to absorption of Christian and Viking strengths). But the source is most important of all, since without a sense of ancient identity (through song, story and ritual), as the Master tells Aniel at the end, the folk 'feel that by going forward they leave their true riches behind'.

The Grove is their primeval sun circle. There is a heart of darkness here, one in which Gunn does not avoid the horror, but one where out of horror also comes life, purged and renewed. Gilbrude is the anachronistic aspect of the Grove, the Master, the adapting consciousness who recognizes that the ancient ways have come to a great turning-point, one of those turns of the cycle Yeats called 'gyres'. The idea of sacrifice dominates this novel, through the haunting presence and threat of the Grove. With an ambivalence similar to that of Gibbon in his images of standing stones in *Sunset Song* (1932), Gunn pursues the heart of the Grove's mystery – a mystery of complexity of mind rather than of the supernatural. What needs did the sacrifice assuage? Were some of the victims – as Breeta herself here, caught up in the plight of the tribe – even willing? What utterly alien thought processes moved Gilbrude, the Druids, the folk? The novel attempts to explore that alien territory in a way no other work of Scottish – perhaps English – literature has attempted. Gunn concludes that with the destruction by fire of the Grove, the Master recognizes the finality of change: 'It is finished.' The biblical echo is intentional, the phrase highly significant throughout Gunn's work, in its profound ambiguity.

The phrase carries two opposed meanings. First, it is tragic, signifying the doom of a way of life. But there is a deeper, and strangely affirmative meaning, signifying ending because the work, of art or of life, is complete, properly finished. This the Master sees; in its profundity of meaning, its implication that out of tragedy comes renewal or renaissance, lies Gunn's deepest meaning. In the heart of despair lies what *Butcher's Broom* will call 'a hostile happiness'. No lesser insight can console the tragedy of Scotland's folk in their repeated cataclysms. But the Master also identifies the legacy of such a cyclic tragedy. Gunn's most used word, in all its variations, is 'fated'; as 'fey', 'fatalistic', 'fatal' or 'fatalism', becoming the motif of hopeless generations from *Sun Circle* onwards. Its hypnotic use in all these major novels should tell us what is his final diagnosis of the Scottish folk condition – that despair has taken on its own life or rhythm, locking will and character into an expectation of tragedy. From *Sun Circle* on, Gunn seeks to challenge that fatal rhythm, that Scottish *anomie* or *aboulia* (to borrow MacDiarmid's terms), and to show that endurance and resilience can break the black circle of defeatism.

Aniel and Breeta discover love and wild joy amidst Viking carnage; Nessa finds a kind of fulfilment even in her death; the musician Leu's pipe (taken originally from an even older tribe than the Ravens) is taken back, to make new music reflecting the turn of night to day. Leu's name, an echo of that of the ancient Celtic sun god, is used just as later characters are given Ossianic names like Finn, Bran, or Luath. And Leu's death symbolizes the death of an older mythic cycle, which will be supplanted in *Butcher's Broom* by the Fiann legends. So too does the death of the great White Bull in the cleansing, revolutionary fire which destroys the Grove and old ways of life at the end. It is finished also; but 'it was a satisfying end for the old bull, driven out by the younger bulls . . . His prime had been too splendid . . .' Aniel's future telling of the bull's death will create legend, in its contributing to mythology.

Thus, very early in his development, Gunn begins his great statement about the regenerative nature and function of art in Scottish community – and community universally. Here, as in all the epic novels, we are considering, story, song and dance evolve out of life itself – from a defeat, a great natural event (like the death of the white bull), the rhythms of seasonal and regular activities, from the making of fire, to the lamenting of the dead. At the heart of the Ravens' circle is 'a cycle of stories whereby all the ways of tragedy were traced out'. A final understanding of Gunn's work will elude the reader if the magical transcendence of tragedy is not seen as emerging either from the therapeutic rituals of ceilidh and dance, or through a contact with the wholeness of natural background which draws much from Wordsworth, but in the end argues more simply that both art and immediate consolation come from an ancient and animistic relation with the earth itself. From the beginning of this novel, with Aniel's ever more insistent urges to carve and paint the unknown, to the final chapters of *The Silver Darlings*, Gunn shows what he sees as the essential, abiding function of art. Its luminous radiance from self to community is Gunn's most subtle variation of the metaphor of 'sun circle'.

And the relationship between the Master and Aniel shows the underlying way the meaning of art is passed on. It is no accident that the Master is described frequently as 'brown as the hazel', anticipating *Young Art* and *The Green Isle* in their use of the legend of the hazelnuts of knowledge which, falling into the river of life, are eaten by the salmon which becomes the body of wisdom itself (in its turn eaten by Finn McCoull). The Master is a part of that legend, and of the art which will change and develop the meanings, metaphors and legends constantly. The Master is almost the 'collective unconscious' of his race. Aniel tells Breeta 'he can sit down and think . . . back through the life before' (Aniel in turn is learning from him how to do this). Gunn leaves it open how far we read this 'thinking' as metaphor for imaginative empathy for other times, other states, or whether a variation on 'second sight' (so central to *Butcher's Broom* and *The Silver Darlings*) is being suggested. Certainly it is significant that the Master foresees fire in the strath in the ages to come, just as Seumus Og in *Butcher's Broom* 'sees' the Clearances. The Master foresees both the regeneration of the race after the Viking horror and the future disruption once again of the sun circle through Clearance. Thus Gunn forges the links of theme and motif through his trilogy. Several times in the novel Gunn even looks forward to *Young Art and Old Hector*, as he emphasizes how special the hazel tree is for youth and age. It is the tree of age because it carries 'the nuts of divination and wisdom', but 'is also a boy's tree, because no other tree sends up such straight young shoots'. And Gunn asks, 'Do age and youth meet here – the wisdom that must become as a little child? . . . between the lovely straight shoots of youth and the final nuts of wisdom, what is there, after all, but growth of wood?' The relationship between Aniel and the Master which thus begins Gunn's epic work, consistently ends it in the even more essential form of the relationship between young Art and old Hector.

But much has to happen – much wood to be grown – between the first and last simplicities. Gunn has started on a personal quest, and the sly pun in the name of Aniel is the first of many. Thus Neil Gunn will find himself at the start of a quest, like Aniel at the end of the novel, and Gunn's continuation of the quest will be shown in the variations of Gunn tribal names in later novels, and in the central role given to the Gunns thereby. Two ancient presences come out of *Sun Circle* to the future. The ancient people of the hinterland, older by far than the Ravens, the Finlags, have a mysterious role. Are they the little people (for they are wee and elusive, elflike in themselves and their houses and weapons), the originals of the 'Sidhe na Danaan', whose echoes will be heard throughout the epic novels? Within their name is future legendary naming, perhaps leading to Finn of *The Silver Darlings*, Gunn's final hero, descended from the heart of the sun circle Picts, the oldest folk of all. Finn, after all, will have his vision of the Master at the centre of the House of Peace. And, moreover, Drust has another son, enchantingly conceived in his love with the Dark Woman of the Finlags, the Black Hind. Gunn sees this as carrying future import – else why have 'Breeta and [Aniel] offering homage to that small dark woman of the Finlags and her small son'? There is an open face of history, but, says Gunn, there is also a mysterious hidden face, and it looks in secret down through the ages. It may even look from the Black Hind to Dark Mairi of the Shore in *Butcher's Broom*: Mairi's origins are deliberately made uncertain, but she is 'an inland woman' of the enduring kind found in the oldest places, and granddaughter of Black MacIver, a legendary Caithness smuggler. Her line of descent is very old and dark – she is, finally, Mairi Sutherland, eponymous spirit of her race.

Butcher's Broom has an arresting title with jarring, arcane significances. Gunn means it so. The 'butcher' is in one sense the Duke of Cumberland, German leader of the genocidal Hanoverian troops at Culloden and after, and his 'broom' swept thousands of Highlanders to death and exile, and made rubbish of their culture and identity. This is thus the breaking once more of the 'sun circle' (often used as metaphor through this novel) of community which has regenerated itself and endured for another millennium. We are to witness yet again the intrusion of vast impersonal forces into a simple, good community; though this time the enemies will be more insidious than directly hostile Vikings or well-meaning missionaries. Gunn was now deeply involved in nationalist politics, and it is important to read (just as it is with Naomi Mitchison's *The Bull Calves* (1947) a decade later) a double reference throughout, to the ancient past and to modern Scotland, in two time planes simultaneously. Gunn and Gibbon were in letter contact after the book appeared. Gibbon shared Gunn's anger at the plight of the common people of Scotland. Gunn wrote to him that 'the poor seem to obsess us both', and it is in this sense of the timeless plight of ordinary people confused in their identity and as to their survival that the novel should be read. The other meaning(s) of 'Butcher's Broom' refer again to the secret face of history. The name is the folk-name for *Ruscus aculeatus*, or box holly – an ancient cleansing and tonic plant, disused now because the skill in handling its bitter and its poisonous aspects is lost. It would be one of Dark Mairi's regenerative herbs, such as we see her employing at the symbolic opening of the novel, when she purges the toxins from a sick man. Like Scott's Jeanie Deans, she is an archetype of regeneration; and as with Scott's novel, there is a polar opposite to her, in the authoritarian forces of centralized society which, using Cumberland as a tool, will negate her traditional society. Gunn's is the darker vision, however. Mairi will be destroyed by the sheepdogs of the Sassenach shepherds, just as her people will be. The local tacksman's wife will throw the sprig of butcher's broom (which is also to be the badge of her clan) into the fire, as formal resignation of family honour. The chief has become an absentee, who no longer identifies with his kin, preferring to allow them to be exiled, and the land cleared instead for sheep. It is a terrible story, as Gibbon said to Gunn. But is it a tragedy?

The Ravens have become the people of the Riasgan, as the Master foresaw. The first half of the book shows that – despite ominous signs – the 'sun circle' of their ceilidhs, their glen, their life, is again rich and light-filled. Gunn's descriptions subtly use the circle image again and again so that even the waulking of cloth is performed in a sunwise circle, turning like a 'mythical serpent'. Thus links with the past are woven, just as frequent storytelling recalls that old world with 'wolves and bears and boars and beasts like little lions . . . and . . . beasts like hairy men'. The reader will recall the lynx which terrified Breeta, and the Ravens' mockery of the hairy Finlags. To this has been added the legends of Finn and Cuchulain and Deirdre, and a wonderful sun-poetry which blesses the little streams and the grassy hillocks; again, the reader will find this in *The Silver Darlings* blended with the twenty-third psalm's green pastures and still waters, but descended and continuous from that first circle. The 'Ancient Bard' credited with many of these could well be a descendant of Aniel and his father Taran (and we should always remember the sly identification of Neil Gunn himself with that continuity), so that the storyteller is at once old Angus Sutherland, the voice of Sutherland itself speaking through the ages, as much as Neil Gunn, descendant of Aniel.

For the novel is about Scotland as well as Sutherland. As the danger signs of troop-raising for the Napoleonic Wars grow, the tone of the book grows grimmer, and a chill enters, literally: ' . . . a chill night wind from the south . . . searching along the backbone and between the ribs of ancient Alba, searching up . . . the game of death . . .' When Mairi's adopted 'daughter', Elie, wanders through the starving Lowlands with her illegitimate son Colin (her lover Colin having answered the chief's call for volunteers for the war), Gunn is clearly calling on Hugh Miller's radical essays on the Highlands, and particularly *My Schools and Schoolmasters* (1853), and presents a savage and sympathetic picture of vagrancy, and the poverty of bonded and enslaved workers like the Lowland coalminers, which T.C. Smout's pioneering and fiercely critical *A Century of the Scottish People* (1986) is hard put to rival. Gunn knows Miller, and the state of suffering Scotland of the nineteenth century.

Once again the key word is 'fatal', with all its variations, and now darker by far. Betrayal by the clan chief is Gunn's main target. Here, at the heart of an older, humanistic Scotland, lies the unspeakable; that the leader, who is of the tribe, should separate himself from them for a house in Bond Street, rack-rents, and a pair of overdressed showy Highlanders at his door to impress all London, at the very time he and British law are assiduously destroying these very Highlanders. Perhaps Aniel's journey to Inverness to find a southern son of Drust was *Sun Circle*'s ultimate mistake, the final tragedy of Aniel's people being that they have no ability to lead, since they don't understand the concept of hierarchy. After all, Aniel's most instinctive and powerful vision was of Nessa and Haakon the Viking becoming an intermarried Pictish-Viking leadership, but the fatalism of his tribesmen destroyed this. Is the fatal flaw of Celt and Scot thus endemic, inherent, a genetic doom? Gunn is being savage here – Aniel's failure, Colin's acceptance of the chief's treachery (for Colin and Elie are the descendants of Aniel and Breeta), the childish bluster of the Riasgan – all exemplify a Celtic and Scottish proclivity for defeat, what Gunn describes in the culminating chapters of the book as shameful, 'a recognition of some inner futility and weakness in their character, a fatal central dividing within them, paralyzing all power of decisive action'. Gunn's contempt for those of his race who accept Celtic Twilight cliché reaches its highest here, in chapter 2, part 3, with his picture of the young Highlander Davie's vituperative 'Children of the Gael! Children of the tempest! Children!' Davie's perception of a dangerous infantilism in their debased images of themselves is also Gunn's mockery of the Celtic Twilight and the Kailyard literary school, of Fiona Macleod and particularly of Neil Munro's *Children of Tempest* (1903), full of stereotypes which *Butcher's Broom* continually satirizes.

For Gunn sees this as the time of the spiritual deformation of the Highlands, when women took over the guardianship of the communities from men, since the forces which are destroying the community have drained them of men and of their essential manhood. Now is when Gaelic becomes seen by predatory outsiders as the language of feckless, devious and idle Highlanders, and the stereotypes of drunken unreliability are created. Gunn shows (outstandingly, in his portrayal of the spiritual disintegration of Rob the Miller) the grim, enervating reality of fatalism and loss of hope.

In *The Green Isle* Gunn will show that God has withdrawn from his people; and indeed Gunn suggests here that there is a curse upon them, such is their agony. Not, of course, a curse such as the Church suggests, because of their pagan ways: Gunn mocks this, seeing the Church's role in the Clearances as collaborative with landed interest and exploitation. Gunn's motif for landlord treatment of tenants and communities is that of Christ before Caiaphas. The modern agents have names like Heller (Sellars?) and Falcon, indicative of their rapine. Again, we remember that this novel is about Scotland. Heller is the archetype of the new materialism of the Lowland Scot, with 'the hard bone in his cheek and jaw, . . . the set of his mouth'. The Countess of Sutherland recognizes his type, since she 'had been brought up in the Lowlands of Scotland by her grandmother, a scheming worldly woman . . . they could be harder than the bone in their faces.' As with Culloden, the destruction of the older Scotland is mainly brought about by dark forces within Scotland itself.

The Riasgan has a last golden summer before its destruction. It is all the more striking since Gunn sets it within a context of gathering greyness and ominous change. This last summer is fated and diseased. References to the 'Aged Bard' and to the great pibroch 'The Lament for the Children' by the doomed pipers, the MacCrimmons, are all shot through with bitterness and parody. The community corrodes from within, the men's ineffectuality rotting their self-respect. All this is summed up in the Riasgan's last wedding, the corrupt marriage of Elic to Rob the Miller. It is a union which should never have been, attended by sniggers and despair, unspoken reservations and the worst kind of fatalism: on Elie's part from the need to protect her bastard child, on Rob's because deep down he knows of the essential wrongness of the marriage. It is the sign of the Riasgan's loss of wholeness, and of its healing arts. Significantly, it is the boy Davie – heir to the Finlags – who sees that in condoning the union, the community has lost its instinctive rightness: 'they had handed her over.' We are reminded of Breeta's becoming scapegoat, sacrificial victim for the ills of community, a thousand years before. It was wrong then; it is as wrong now.

There is a choric figure to pass judgment, savage and embittered, on all this. Tomas MacHamish the cattle-drover has an epic role to play. Sharp observer at any time, he is enlarged through tragedy to mythic scale, becoming the frenzied daemon of his race's despair. Boldly Gunn has him cite Tacitus as comment on the atrocities of government ('where they make a desert, they call it peace') and invoking the ancient spirit of Galgacus, leader of the Picts in ancient time against the Romans. What deepens Tomas's ironic role is the realization that such noble resistance and high ideals are now pointless and misplaced, since (as the bitter cripple Murdoch, symbol of the deformed modern Highlands, sees) there are no simple enemies such as Roman or Viking, but more insidious enemies mainly within their community, like the absentee chief, their own loss of hope, and the ironically misplaced trust they are conditioned to give. Similarly epic is Tomas's central vision of the cloven-footed presence which will destroy them. Gunn fuses wild humour and deep satire in Tomas's invocation of the Ram as Destroyer; true, since sheep will replace humanity, and effective, since biblical and pagan echoes attend the Pan-Devil figure. Tomas, 'as the last living witness to Galgacus and Ossian', is given the right to utter the final curse – and its savagery, coming from a gentle and chief-trusting people, will be obvious. Now 'a veritable doubled-up rag of a man, with burning eyes and pointed skeleton-arms', Tomas gives voice to Gunn's repeated attack on vast, impersonal, and centralized power, whether that of imperial Britain, with press-gang and law court, or later in totalitarian Russia or Hitler's Germany. It is 'law' which allows the chief to clear the people. In the face of this irony, Tomas suggests that the folk should thank chief and authorities for allowing them to rot on their sea-beaches. Then, abandoning sarcasm, Tomas deepens his satire by suggesting that at least the slave-trader 'traffics honestly in human bodies, and enlists the aid neither of Progress nor of Jesus Christ'. The Countess of Sutherland is worse – not because she has abandoned the ways of her forefathers – many have; but

> . . . I am cursing her now not for dispossessing the people of their own land, not for having made the law that gave her the power to dispossess her own people, not for having burned them out of their ancient homes, not for having made them wanderers and beggars and eaters of filth, not for the angels of insanity and disease and death she sent amongst them, not even for having tried to justify herself in the eyes of the world by employing an army, by using Christ's Church, by weighting the balances of justice . . . but because in using all these things . . . she has broken the spirit of her people, she has destroyed the soul of her people; as surely as if she were Judas, she has crucified the Gael.

Is there any doubting Gunn's passion, his epic anger about his race? This is himself speaking, and it has the anger quality and intensity of Swift in *A Modest Proposal* (1729). It is Gunn at his darkest and finest – yet even here it is only part of a bigger regeneration. For even here, as British political cunning reaches new depths in setting Irish regiments, who have suffered Highland depredation in their country, against their old enemies in enforcing the Clearances, Celt against Celt, equally victims of southern duplicity – even here at the heart of darkness Gunn regenerates the old myths, re-creating them to offer hope and ancient strength to Scotland.

It is the old trick, whereby an ancient resilience reasserts itself. It was at the heart of the book, when Elie, utterly lost and hopeless, found that mysterious 'hostile happiness' amidst a wintry, bleak landscape, or where Dark Mairi, smooring the fire on the brink of Clearance, finds meaning beyond tragedy in the traditional blessing of the hearth. Mairi is endurance, beyond tragedy, and a reading of her terrible death as tragic is simply wrong. 'It is finished'; the Master of *Sun Circle* recognized the finality of his work, and Mairi Sutherland is fitly his successor. It is Mairi who is seen as the real knotting of history; she herself would not recognize defeat in her own death. Thus Gunn tells his race that they are never, and have never been, truly defeated. The fire is smoored, but not out.

In all this the links with *Sun Circle* have been strongly made. Not only does Mairi follow the Master; not only are Elie and Colin latterday and fallen Breeta and Aniel; Tomas has kept lore and legend alive ('Fingal never fought a fight without offering terms'), from even before the Ravens' time. With the occasional fragmented memories of the 'nameless ones', Dark Gods of the Night Wind, or the glimpse of fairy lore, we see that these are descendants of Ravens and Finlags. Even the breaking of the circle of the Riasgan is not final. Gunn tells us that these people are endurers, greater than all the leaders who come and go, transient and irrelevant to them. And it is important to see that the links forward to *The Silver Darlings* have been made likewise. Catrine, like Elie, will be 'fey', arid and alone, yet will find her own 'hostile happiness'; and she will moreover be married to a descendant of the MacHamishes, who have featured significantly here. Tomas the Drover was a MacHamish ('a sept of the Gunns, thoroughly godless dangerous ruffians', Gunn slyly has Mr Falcon comment); there's a 'black giant', a friend of Rob, also a MacHamish; and the traditional community piper is of the sept. This will be the pedigree of young Finn of *The Silver Darlings*: their energy, awareness of tradition, and centrality to community will be his. (There's even –

looking beyond to the later novels – a 'young Art, who is thirteen and a leader'!)

Butcher's Broom held at its centre the assertion of a profound natural endurance, with its central location of Dark Mairi discovering affirmation at the heart of negation. The next movement in the quest for the sources of Scottish spiritual regeneration naturally called for a shift of emphasis from the large-scale diagnosis of groups like the Ravens or the Riasgan to the analysis of private self. Gunn's location of new hope in the boy Hugh in *Morning Tide* was based on the idea that in the awakening of the private self in the child and adolescent, tragic public history is defeated, since the child perceives and remakes the world anew. Somehow, the insight of *Morning Tide* into the circle of self, with its convincing sensitivity and delicacy, had to be allied with the two epic novels' sense of the sweep of tragic community history. *The Silver Darlings* took Gunn another seven years to write; the hardest challenge of all, since it called for a triumphant and relatively contemporary conclusion to the trilogy of Pictish, Celtic and Scottish spiritual history.

As early as 1933 Gunn revealed (in a letter to MacDiarmid) his recognition of the need to base his conclusions on sound psychological theory. Hating the accusation that his work was ever 'mystical', Gunn saw the essential challenge in the need to reconcile myth, notions of 'Great Memory' or collective unconscious, and instinctive endurance, with rational and practical modern ideology.

> I recognize that where you have a given psychology, like the Scottish, you must deal with it as scientifically as possible in accordance with such rules as advanced psychologists have formulated . . . When an expert like A.S. Neill is dealing with a perverted or sub-normal child he doesn't slam educational facts into the child with the help of a rod, like the old dominie: on the contrary, he apprehends the level of the child mind and makes a point of contact . . .

Significantly, Gunn perceived Scotland as 'perverted' through history, and Neill is chosen as the fittest exemplar of modern psychological understanding. Neill's organic and sympathetic methods in relation to children strongly influenced Gunn's development now, and *Highland*

River (1937) was the 'new phase' through which Gunn had to move to *The Silver Darlings*.

An essay like this cannot deal fully with two of Gunn's greatest novels. I have concentrated on *Sun Circle* and *Butcher's Broom* not because they are greater than the two later works, but because much more critical attention has been given to the latter. I have discussed both fully elsewhere; I can merely stress here that in *Highland River* Gunn stood aside, as it were, from his epic, exploring instead the theme of the child as father of the man in a *Prelude*-like prose-poem which was also an extended meditation on the nature of the discovery of essential self. The influence of natural objects on war-scarred Kenn Sutherland has epic qualities. Kenn discovers in his roots and in his real river's source the origin of natural self forgotten by modern man when the river (of man) took the wrong turning. The 'source' he discovers is a Scottish poise of place and community, with respect for private communion together with a sense of wider involvement. It will supply *The Silver Darlings* with the spiritual insights which illuminate its often tragic history.

The Silver Darlings fuses all Gunn's themes heretofore. There is the satiric commentary on the warping of Scottish and Highland community. There is a continual exploration of legend and myth through song, dance and story. There is an examination of the way tragedy affects individuals: widowed Catrine, Roddie the fisherman, at sea in his emotional life since he cannot fulfil himself; a wonderful range of relationships which Gunn controls and arranges to body forth his grand symphonic design. There is in it a fundamental sense of the pragmatic issues of fishing, the rural economy, trade with the Baltic, gained from his political involvements of the 1930s, his reading of his encourager and friend Peter Anson's books on fishing like *Fishermen and Fishing Ways* (1932), and his own summer of sailing in Scottish coastal waters in 1937, when he made that impulsive leap for freedom (by leaving his employment at HM Customs and Excise) described vividly in *Off in a Boat* (1938). Or was it so impulsive? Was perhaps Gunn's deep insistence on getting his perspectives right, asserting itself 'behind the scenes' prior to tackling *The Silver Darlings?* Certainly that novel's wonderful dualism of perspective, whereby the first movements are seen through the eye of land-based characters like Catrine, and the later movements through the sea-washed vision of

Roddie and Finn, has an authenticity which surely demanded personal experience going beyond the fact that Gunn's father had been a Dunbeath skipper.

In fusing all previous themes, however, there is one which stands out: that of the central figure of the boy in his passage through initiation into community and mature self. Indeed, *Sun Circle's* symbolism is brought triumphantly to a close in the novel's final chapter, 'Finn in the Heart of the Circle', and Finn on the final page is given the last of his glimpses of the Master, 'the white-haired man he had once imagined here'. Is this journey from Master to Finn not in itself proof that Gunn was – however arduous and long the quest – searching for a way of completing the broken circle, so that he could use the phrase 'it is finished' in its most positive sense? Finn, in mastering self, in reconciling himself with mother, community, and his role as husband and father, is Gunn's final and finest exemplar of Scottish spirit triumphing over forces within and without Scotland. Gunn's love and understanding of the child (here perhaps so intense because he was creating the child he and his wife never had) is only rivalled by the insights of *Young Art and Old Hector* – his next book. In this fable of a Scottish childhood, there is more than a real boy, however; Finn has a mythic doppelgänger who accompanies him throughout his childish ploys and adolescent adventures (like his fabulous climb of the Cliff of the Seven Hunters), his dreams (when he has his vision of the great war-horn of Finn, which he has to blow to awaken his sleeping people), and most of all in his art, his achievement of his place in the web of symbols and meanings captured in traditional dance, story and song. The penultimate chapter of the novel, 'As the Rose Grows Merry in Time', draws all the novel's strands together majestically and movingly, as Finn, in North Uist, learns from and participates in the seamless garment of the community's commentary on itself through its three nights of ceilidh. At last he understands his mother and his selfish desire to shun her – because of a song and a dance. He understands himself, because in telling his story of his epic voyage and by singing the song of the challenge of the maiden to her lover to achieve the impossible, he recognizes how actions and situations like his own have become recorded and made into legend and myth, in turn giving traditional identity to later generations. Finn, who 'came from the hills', and is laughed at by the market boys, is a Finlag. His recurrent identification with the House of Peace, relic of his race in the times of the Ravens and before, performs the same function as Chris Guthrie's link with the standing stones in *Sunset Song*. It shows that he is the apotheosis of his race, descendant and hero whose exploits will stand like those of his namesake, the great Finn McCoull. The people create Finn; Finn creates the people – and thus the circle of action and art move inextricably around. Thus Gunn allows the psychological elements of the novel to sit in easy ambivalence with the folk and supernatural elements. Incidences of second sight, of rowanberries performing their healing function, of perceptions transcending time such as Finn often experiences at the House of Peace, are left in a suspension in which Gunn provides perfectly adequate rational explanations – but suggests also that the rational and the supernatural are not so antagonistic as modern materialism insists.

The triumph of the herring fisheries around the coast of Scotland in the nineteenth century stands as Gunn's ultimate example of a model of regeneration of mythic stature. His recurrent description of the times of the silver darlings as 'fabulous', however, doesn't mean that 'magic' has brought about salvation – far from it, since it is essential to his purpose that this Scottish myth also stands as realistic model for the nation which he had told MacDiarmid in 1933 was failing because of 'internal warring elements'. Scott had sought to reconcile these 'internal warring elements', as had others after him; but neither in Scott's main efforts, or anywhere else in Scottish literature – not even in MacDiarmid's *Drunk Man* – does supreme art marry so fruitfully with social and historical authenticity and sensitive and persuasive psychological delineation. *The Silver Darlings* has a claim as the greatest of all Scottish novels; and the trilogy it completes, the quest for a new myth which will (to use the words of the American anthropologist Philip Wheelwright) 'explain the origins and ends of a race to itself', has a claim to mark the highest level of achievement of Scottish and Western literature.

Where would Gunn's epic quest take him thereafter? Later novels like *The Drinking Well* (1946) might explore the contemporary problem of rural Scotland, but could hardly be seen as sequels, since the idea of completion, of a historical circle coming round to the totality of 'it is finished' (as Gunn knew it was, from the vanishing fishing fleets of his father's day) gave that trilogy its integral rhythms. Scott had gone 'out of history' to find Jeanie Deans and a folk model for his vision of abiding Scottish strength. Gunn had developed that model triumphantly so that the centripetal or inward dynamics of Scottish development could be seen as self-generating. But what of the value and nature of these Scottish archetypes in relation to the centrifugal, outward-looking dynamics of Scotland? In terms of modern philosophical and political materialism, in a world darkened by Stalin, Franco and Hitler, of what value could peripheral minutiae and far-flung folklore possibly be?

The answer was of course implicit in all Gunn's previous work. As early as 1958 Kurt Wittig, in his *The Scottish Tradition in Literature*, argued that Gunn 'is looking for the pattern of life, the underlying ritual, the myth' – in short, the meaning of life itself. Gunn himself argued that 'if a Scot is interested in dialectical materialism or proletarian humanism . . . he should study the old system in order to find out how the new system would be likely to work amongst his kind. It might help him at least to get rid of his more idealistic wind.' Significantly, Wittig, in the last extensive chapter in his account of Scottish literature, ended with discussion of *The Green Isle of the Great Deep* and *Highland River*.

The Green Isle is not, however, a work standing on its own. It can be read as such, just as, say, *The Silver Darlings*; but it is immeasurably enriched by being seen as part of a duality, or an archway, half of which is *Young Art and Old Hector*. It is the second part of the adventures of Art and Hector, and the culmination of their relationship. Essentially the two parts make up a single great work of art which addresses new issues from those he has handled before. We are exploring what periphery can offer centre, or how ancient values of simple community must qualify the values of modern scientific rationalism. Having demonstrated how Scots need not accept decline with self-fulfilling fatalism, Gunn presses on here to show that their enduring qualities of traditional community are the missing and essential ingredients of our brave new world.

Young Art nevertheless continues the trilogy quest. Finn had seen himself at the end of the novel as 'a whitehaired old man, head of a tribe, sitting on this knoll in quiet thought, his sea days over'; and, daringly, Gunn will forge links now which will, for the reader who has followed the quest, link and fuse the Master with Finn, with Old Hector – and God himself. How slyly Gunn hides his clues! But look closely, and Hector – at times comic and hairy – is one of the old Finlags, the last of his race, a bridge between unbroken sun circle (his village was the Clash, the Riasgan-like community lost in the Clearances) and the new Highlands of young Art. Circle imagery still performs its linking function. Art's family is 'a circle of peace', blessed by his father's Grace, as were the families of the Riasgan. (Gunn has changed the locale to the west – perhaps to emphasize the archetypal role of his figures, and to avoid the charge of parochialism?) The very first story of the novel (for it is both collection of stories and novel, just as the volume itself is also part of the next novel) echoes the relationship in *Sun Circle* between Aniel and the Master. It does so twice: first in the Art-Hector encounter, and, second, in the consoling story Hector tells the irate little boy about the Druid and Finn McCoull. The Master's teaching persists – and more. The Dark Ones ('who can be vindictive') are still remembered in this nineteenth-century tale, if not as vividly as in *Butcher's Broom*, as are the fairies, their dwellings and their habit of replacing children with changelings. Most of all, however, the older themes are developed towards a new statement of the concept of 'it is finished'. In 'The First and the Second Childhood', Hector finds in the Druid-pupil, innocence-wisdom relationship he has with Art a 'vision of the circle completing itself', so that 'panic or time could no more intrude'. It will be the disgrace of modern rationalism in *The Green Isle* that it cannot accept the magical quality of their relationship, restlessly examining it for hidden motivation or even sick sexual exploitation.

From the outset it is worth knowing that the two novels will contain a shared pattern and movement. Taking the opening of *Young Art* and the end of *Green Isle* together, we see that the movement has been from the Hazel Pool (shades of the Master!) to the Hazel Pool; from Art's desire to find the river to the river itself as end of his quest; from a story of a salmon to the living salmon they bring out of the pool at the end; from the wisdom of the Druid at the beginning to that of God at the end; and, more mundanely, from Morag, Art's sister and her shepherd, Tom, to their crucial role in rescuing Art and Hector at the end. And the shared quest is, quite simply, for wisdom – the heart of the legend of the hazelnuts of knowledge and the magical movement beyond knowledge and rationalism to the mysterious territory beyond. As the imagery of pools held *Highland River* together, so the recurring, tantalizing glimpse of the Hazel Pool unites this work.

The title, of course, is charged with far-reaching meaning. Art is a common name in the north, as is Hector; but seven-year-old Art (like Finn) has his other level of existence, on which he is timeless youth – and particularly Arthur, the young hero-king, who was tutored by the wise old Sir Hector. Gunn exploits the fact that the Arthurian legends are parents to the Celtic Fianns, so that the implication is that the relationship here is older and deeper even than Finn's with the old Druid. But there is another and major new aim in this quest. It is nothing less than to find the heart of the relationship between psychology and myth. In *Young Art* Gunn keeps the two separate, delicately and perceptively analyzing the mutual interests of Art and Hector, while allowing myth to come in through illustrative folk tales (many taken directly from Campbell's famous collection of 1890, *Popular Tales of the Western Highlands*). Reality and legend move intimately, but separately. *The Green Isle* dramatically abolishes the distinction, by moving directly into the shared unconscious of Art and Hector (in their drowning dream at the bottom of the Hazel Pool) to intuit the sources of myth-making. Dream will be seen as the place where reality and myth are synthesized. This is Gunn's triumphant step beyond historical materialism.

If much of the substance of *Young Art* is drawn from legends and children's tales, there is nothing childish about Gunn's exploitation of them. Art will teach Hector (that life is divided into three parts, in 'The Knife, the Glass Ball, and the Penny'), just as much as Hector's stories will lead Art to Finn's wisdom. The role of storytelling is again crucial – even when Art, miserable at the loss of his mother, will not listen to the consoling Hector. How delicately Gunn implies that even 'unheard' stories have their subtle effect: 'though Art did not listen to him, he spoke of the hunter and the hunter's courage and of how Art had now proved himself and would one day be a grown man . . .' And how charmingly he shows the effect of the tales on Art and Donul, his big brother. After hearing of the strange birdbeast and the twelve puppies who ate the youngest daughter's bannock: ' "I thought once or twice," said Art in a quiet voice, "that I just saw

them." "I have thought that myself sometimes," answered Donul . . .'
Each episode is a 'building block' towards the time of testing ahead in
the *Green Isle*. Each will contribute to Art's (and Hector's) resources, so
that a perceptive reading will show that the significance of these
apparently trivial events in *Young Art* is crucial, unfolding into full
meaning later. Each episode calls forth new growth from Art, leading
him to intuitive insights, such as in 'Machinery', when, fascinated, he
watches the terrible teeth of the millwheel's cogs and gears. 'Darkly Art
suspected that this machinery had more in it than men who laughed at
him believed. They had better look out or one day it would catch and
drag them in . . .' Likewise his powers of imagination are being
developed. Art elaborates on details of the birdbeast and puppies to
Donul, telling him, as he grips his hand, 'I thought the birdbeast was
like a great raven, and the puppies were little black puppies.' Gunn lets
us see the virtue of the openness of folk-tale, in allowing much personal
handled visualization, and Art's originality. And the episodes are not
separated – they refer back and forward, and often their full meaning or
subtlety will only emerge much later. For example, in the sensitive
account of Art's resentment of his new brother Henry James, Gunn
plants Art's jealousy without telling us what it is about – or why, much
later, he goes about pale and quiet, wasted by an unnamed guilt. We
learn in a later story that he has implored the fairies to take away Henry
James – and thus, when he hears his mother say that Henry James 'is not
like himself', being ill, he assumes the fairies have visited – and left a
changeling. The notion of Art's jealousy, fairy involvement, and guilt
is sustained over several episodes, and, like Finn's encounter with the
serpent-conger eel in *The Silver Darlings*, is both positive and negative
in his development. It shows him discovering guilt (and becoming
'fey'); but it leads him to the ruined homes of his ancestors, in a lyrical
sequence in which he seeks the old gooseberry bush outside Hector's old
house in the Clash, in a quest which is simultaneously for peace and
knowledge (since Henry James has come from such a bush!). Hector
finds him asleep within the ruins of his (Art's) grandfather's house. The
past is imparting itself to him; like Finn, seeing the Master at the House
of Peace, Art has achieved a kind of epiphany in which he is given
communion with his ancestors. Hector is as astonished to find him as if
he had 'come upon a fearful and fabulous beast, sunning itself in an
unexpected place'.

This is the central epiphany of the first volume. It marks Art as special, and, like Hector, a leader of his people – as *The Green Isle* will demonstrate. But lesser and magical epiphanies surround it. Probably the next in the scale of importance are respectively 'Art Runs a Great Race' and 'Art's Wedding Present'. In the first, Art is out of himself with excitement at the local games, and never more so than when he bursts himself to win his race. His feat will stand him in good stead in *The Green Isle*; and we will meet the 'starter from Clachdrum' again . . . In 'Art's Wedding Present', Art comes of age by saving Hector from prison when he discovers the excisemen sniffing up the glen for illicit distilling. Hector is an old hand in this, and has his secret den in a hillock where his 'worm' distils whisky. Art saves the wedding of his brother, the whisky for it, and Hector; Hector says that all that remains ' "is for you to hold it *as secret as the grave* . . ." "As secret as the grave", murmured Art, his heart like to burst with the amount of life and loyalty in it.' Gunn ends with a sly pun. Hector's delight is great. 'I was beginning to think we had hidden the old worm too well . . .' But there's more than Art proving himself in his community. Hector's den is also 'Knocshee', *cnoc na sidhe*, the fairy hill; and Hector its magical inhabitant, as in the astonishing moment when Art comes upon him emerging, the hairy *oorishk* itself, the fabulous beast-human, from his den. Is this where legends are born? (And were trolls and the like hidden humans, from smugglers to persecuted Covenanters?) For Art, magic, fable and reality combine to implant – beyond all reach of the inquisitors of the Green Isle's totalitarian state – fundamental goodness and strength. Everything he's heard – older discussions about the Clearances, about property, about loyalty; and everything that's happened, down to his wonderful moment when he gets his first knife – will fulfil its purpose in the Green Isle.

There is one apparent drawback to this unified design. Some stories, notably that about his brother Donul going off to work far away, 'The Little Red Cow', are not about Art or Hector. What have Donul, or the red cow he looks after in the south, to do with the totality of *Young Art* and *The Green Isle of the Great Deep*? In fact, this is one of Gunn's most subtle pieces of oblique comment on the essential spirit of his race. The small, shaggy red cow with her fiery eyes and wild unhappiness is the tormented and displaced Celt; commenting on her dourness, the cattleman remarks that 'they're like that, them that come from the West.' The discussion that follows is really about Donul, Art's brother – who intuitively knows what the little cow feels, since she's like his own and Hector's cattle at home, and part of the feeling community. Indeed, a whole way of life goes with the intimate milking and herding of her kind. And in a sense Gunn foreshadows *The Green Isle* in placing Donul in a planned, ultra-rational system where his and the cow's ways are redundant and wasteful – as perceived by the new world. Donul will write home and Art will hear and understand his predicament. Thus *The Green Isle* consists essentially of Art's drowning dream, haunted by all the things he has experienced in the earlier part, but especially moved by the sense of his brother in a strange country, far from home. *The Green Isle* opens with the comic rescue of just such a little red cow.

The Green Isle starts like another episode of *Young Art*. Here – with the fun and sensitivity of *Butcher's Broom* – is community in harmony, till the talk turns to totalitarian methods of brainwashing and concentration camps. To them it is worse than the Clearances, since the breaking of the mind, as Hector makes them all see, is the worst atrocity of all. Art is, of course, drinking all this in. When Red Dougal asks why God does not interfere, we can imagine how – as Gunn stresses – Art's and their minds are haunted. Art and Hector fall into the Hazel Pool, and they fall into a dream, a fable, a sustained meditation – or into an enchanted world – in which emphasis will be given to their most recent and vivid experiences, both of the first chapter 'The Night Before', and of *Young Art*, the first part of the duality.

The dream is ambivalent. It is psychologically explicable, in terms of theories of one's past life flashing before one at the point of death, and stories like Golding's *Pincher Martin* or Bierce's 'Incident at Owl Creek' in which entire extended experience is made the hallucinatory matter of the text. It is also fabulous; since Art has the hazelnuts of knowledge in his pocket, which he takes with him into the river of life, he becomes part of the legendary quest for wisdom. Gunn again posits the idea that traditional art and psychological development, 'magic' and realism, are one; and the aim of Gunn's final epic quest here is to show how the apparently trivial but dogged endurance of such as Hector and Art – a strength of Scottish (or any) traditional community life – can confound all Utopian totalitarianism, and expose its transition to Dystopia.

It is also much more. Gunn has given several differing accounts of the genesis of the novel. In one version it was a nephew of a friend who prompted the book, as though a type of Art himself had suggested it; in another, Naomi Mitchison's disbelief in the authenticity of the Art-Hector relationship, the importance of a Highland strath or its problems is supposed to have led him to this surrealist yet satiric fantasy . Certainly it shows him deliberately entering the territory of Huxley's *Brave New World* (1932) and the later *Nineteen Eighty-Four* (1949) of Orwell, and doing so with a success which cries out to have the novel seen alongside these as modern satire on new social orders of the West. But, more simply, it was the natural development into speculative myth after *Young Art*; all the positive groundwork there insists on some final test, some meta-legend, set against modern negativity, to complete the epic quest.

For the Green Isle, with bluer than earthly waters and greener than earthly fields, into which Art and Hector fall, is a daring fusion of Tir-nan-Og, the Celtic paradise, with nightmare vision of how modern totalitarianism cannot allow individualism. Gunn had always fused pagan and Christian elements in his work. This is the culminating example of his interweaving, so that Celtic and Christian heaven are one, but now eroded by modern materialism and scientific rationalism generally, and totalitarian social conditioning particularly. Dis-entangling the elements of pagan-Christian belief can be difficult: for example, there is a play on 'no room at the inn', in that Art and Hector are expected on arrival in this new land to go dutifully to the inns, and their refusal to go is precisely because there is now too much of the wrong kind of 'room at the inn', so that the arrivals who eat the treated food there become automatons, hooded and sinister 'pilgrims', processed into the new 'perfection' where a kind of authoritarian utilitarianism has come to rule. Man has taken over from God, the overseeing of order, through Inquisitors, at the central cities of each region. The fruit on the trees of the countryside is not to be eaten. Gunn works a strange variation on the taboo on the Tree of Knowledge of Eden, hardly following Christian practice, but in a way which suggests that Christianity and pagan mythology have truth somewhere in both of them. But just as no single authoritarian interpretation of life's meaning is allowed to hold sway in Gunn's work, so the very point here is that it is the wonder of Christian image amd myth which matters, not its dogma. Gunn argues that dogma destroys, just as the dogmatic 'atomic psychology' of the Inquisitors at the seats of power destroys poetry, fun, real laughter, spontaneous delight. (Gunn will later place his analysis of *The Atom of Delight* directly against such destructive analysis.) His picture of the 'perfect society' is chilling; the monotonous singing of 'Three Blind Mice' by disciplined infants, the curious superficial expressions of the people of the isle, which Art hates, the menace of officials, all the more effective since overt violence is absent, and instead they act with an absolute self-confidence arising from total power and control. Art and Hector are indeed welcome in this centralized, categorized society. The Inquisitors and their helpers, like ambitious young Merk and Axel, relish the idea of taking them to pieces to find out what ancient and atavistic primitivism moves them. They are a cerebral challenge, as in a game of chess, the prey of an intellectual hunt.

Art and Hector are not alone in their resistance, however. Some peasants – notably Mary and Robert – are helpful, if reluctantly, as though their instincts are at war with their calculations. Mary lost her child on earth, and Robert, protective to excess, is a failed poet. (There is the gentlest of hints that they are Mary Campbell and Robert Burns, finally united in the Green Isle, but now distorted by heaven's warping.) Besides, Mary comes from the same stock as Hector, and they are both descended from Mairi Ross of generations ago. (Could this be Dark Mairi of *Butcher's Broom*, thus giving continuity from *Butcher's Broom* of *dramatis personae* as well as values?) Mary cannot ignore the claim of kin – or humanity. Art awakens her maternal instinct, as Hector awakens the spirit of hospitality. (It is a sign of how far basic community values and Christianity have been lost on the Green Isle, that they tell their visitors that it is 'not our business to feed the stranger here' – cardinal sin by the lights of any traditional culture!) Hector's Grace – formal and informal – continues the awakening. We should realize, however, that in a sense their awakening had already begun. Mary, Robert, and friends do not eat the processed food which kills individualism. Mary (like Mairi before her) has ancient herbal skills which she uses (in her tart green jelly) to restore the ability to eat the fruit of the Tree of Life after being programmed to eat only the synthetic fodder. As in all the great heroic legends, the heroes have come when their hour is right. God works, as Hector says, in strange ways. And is there perhaps the suggestion that Mary and Robert are kin to Mary and Joseph? Their roles are almost as crucial as those of Art and Hector.

God's ways are even stranger when we consider that Art *is* art; creativity, rumour leading to legend, fable. For Art goes on to run, accompanied by the great dogs (with names from Ossianic legend), so that his elusive fleetness becomes a wonder throughout the Green Isle, and he becomes 'a fabulous youth', an archetype of freedom, energy, disorder and fun. He grows in the telling, too, so that (as well as actually appearing to become a twelve- or thirteen-year-old in this place where time and light can play strange tricks) he becomes Cuchulain (Art's favourite, as was revealed to us in the very first story of *Young Art and Old Hector*), or the epitome of all great hero-rebels. Gunn now synthesizes all previous elements of his epic fiction, so that Art becomes the elusive meaning of life itself, for everybody in the book – including the Inquisitors, since unless they can pin him down, their own meaning and authority will be invalidated. The latent cruelty of the Inquisitors is revealed as their ruthless Hunt develops.

Since ultimate significance is thus invested, in defiance of all conventional modern values, in a boy and an old man, we are prepared for the breathtaking audacity of Gunn's final involvement of God himself. Art, on the run yet again, after being recaptured, stumbles on Hector – but it is not. He is uncannily like him, but this old peasant is, if similarly wise, a bit faster and more resourceful. They run together – after Art has tested God's credentials against the yardstick of home and Hector and Clachdrum. For God it is, and rumour, started by Art and Hector, and Hector's final demand to see him, have called him from his meditations. What is Gunn meaning here? And is the visualization of God not bound to be bathetic and irrational, in that he is too human here? Does this not raise the question as to why God abandoned his heaven (and, by implication by Gunn, his earth) in the first place?

Well, it is after all Art's dream, which is irrational anyway. In a sense, Gunn seeks a sublime bathos, whereby he insists that if God is not made in the image of Hector, and Hector in the image of God, then all he has been arguing through his epic novels is pointless. Myth is created by the human imagination and art. In turn, that myth creates new generations of the folk who re-enact the varieties of the myth. God is man, and man is God – and Gunn sees nothing blasphemous or odd about that. It is a simpler idea than, say Coleridge's notion of the esemplastic imagination, or 'divine creativity', and available to the simplest community. Gunn can go no further in this direction. Hector is the last of his race, he 'is finished', as he tells Art throughout their relationship; not 'finished' in hope or resilience, but rather in the completeness of his life. He knows his people's history, the straths, their streams and their living things. He teaches Art that he (and Art as human process) need look no further than the immediate human locality for beauty and meaning. This noble and wise man did this throughout *Young Art*, and his hero-king, Art, fulfils his teaching by finding God and saving his people – a role which is, as Jessie Weston identified in *From Ritual to Romance* (1920), the basic and abiding archetype of all religious mythology.

But Hector has a crucial role in the Green Isle too. He is caught, early on. He is tempted to give in to the endless questioning, to let his spirit fail; but the reader should not miss the fact that it is the conflict of loyalties and the fear of hurting Mary and Robert, the strangers who took them in, which primarily motivates his temporary – and conditional – surrender. Like old Jeems in *The Grey Coast*, however, there is that in Hector which is wily, elusive and primordial, which will instinctively find ways of resisting even when not appearing to resist. Only when at bay, like some hunted beast, does Hector directly insist on his right to see God. That old-fashioned and unheard-of exercise of right is the final factor in the regeneration of the Green Isle and the transformation of its Dystopia. Gunn's handling of the meeting of God and Hector is pitched perfectly. The two are mirror-images of each other, though Hector's reverence for creation does not let him see that God is himself, talking in dream.

For we return to the fact that all this is Art's – and Hector's – dream. What can they find to talk about? asks Morag fondly, as she and Tom watch the pair they have saved from drowning stop, rapt in conversation. Gunn implies that they are comparing dreams, and that the ultimate condition of a shared 'second sight' has been achieved. And when we bear this in mind, curious aspects of their stay in the Green Isle emerge into the front of our minds – Hector's occasional dizziness throughout, the references to the fluctuations of the 'psychic barometer' (a kind of measure of the intensity of their dream?), continual pseudo-recognition or identifications of characters from the real world – so that Morag (as Mavis) and Tom are here, falling in love, acting under new personae, but still essentially themselves. Robert and Mary are older archetypes, from 'collective unconscious' memories, but Art's use of his new knife, his discovery of the hazelnuts of knowledge in his pockets, when *in extremis* with God, his references to the Clachdrum Games, and his identification of God as the Starter of the Great Race (which he won, and wins again here), these show that 'reality' is working in their drowning minds, as they lie at the bottom of the Hazel Pool. How typical of Art's imagination, his love of Cuchulain's heroism, that God should exit from the dream and the festivities at the regeneration of the Green Isle with the most fabulous long-jump!

But 'reality' can be seen crowding in as the story begins to climax. Axel has a mouth like a pike, people look like eels and Sweet Innocence, the horrifyingly unnatural girl guerrilla, is a haddock; and the closing chapters have a green underwater tinge, together with a roaring in Hector's ears which suggests their rescue by Tom and their emergence from the Hazel Pool. Hector meets God in 'a vast sea-green cavern'. Isn't Gunn suggesting that 'heaven' is here and now, and in the mind? Hector said as much to Mary when they talked about the final goodness of a good harvest. The distortion of man, through industrialization and mental disintegration, is the real fall; in this Gunn is utterly at one with the poet Edwin Muir.

In the end all Gunn's meaning lies in the idea of the Fruit of the Land, and the novel's ubiquitous symbolism of living and eating naturally off the land. The Hazelnuts of Knowledge are thus triumphant over Eden's Tree of Knowledge; Gunn prefers that Art should find the wisdom of Finn McCoull through finding the salmon in the Hazel Pool which has eaten the nuts and thus, swimming in the river of life, gives wisdom to man. It is also a very real salmon in a Scottish river which they bring back with them. They have been to paradise, and come back with the realization that it can be, indeed is Scotland, their landscape, their community, potentially. Read like this, Hector's insistence on seeing God is the end-point of Gunn's quest for essential Scotland. This old man, about to die in his remote landscape, is the meaning of his country, and the finest fruit, just as was Mary, and, in his reawakened poetry, her husband Robert.

Gunn will go on to explore depths of self and complexities of meaning, in profound novels like *The Other Landscape* (1954) and the spiritual autobiography *The Atom of Delight* (1956). But his great epic phase is complete; it is finished. His trilogy and duality have drawn a circle around Neil Gunn's country, giving it the regenerative mythology lost for so long. Gunn's epic fiction is not overtly political. He kept his nationalistic activities by and large separate from his novels. But by asserting the great age and essential resilience of Scottish community spirit, Gunn gives back perspective to Scottish literature and culture, and urges rejection of that fatalism and apathy induced by three hundred years and more of recurrent failure of will at national and local level. The enduring memory of these novels is of resilient women, strong as their land around them, like Breeta and Dark Mairi and Catrine and Mary Campbell; and forward-looking men like Aniel, Colin Sutherland, Finn and Art, standing on the threshold of their adventure, armed only with a sense of their past, and their will to make the present – and, of course, the wisdom of old Hector, the quiet Master of their country's knowledge, the wisdom and knowledge of Neil Gunn himself.

LIVING AROUND WITH NEIL

LIVING AROUND
WITH NEIL

Naomi Mitchison

IT WAS 1941 when I first wrote a rather formal letter to
Neil Gunn, the beginning of a correspondence that went on, more
like a conversation – but then we were both skilled writers, enjoying
our craft – for years and years. Most of our letters are now in the
National Library in Edinburgh and have a lot to tell those who worry
about the future of Scotland. For we were always sliding off into
politics, however we started. They have been used by other writers
about Neil Gunn, especially Hart and Pick in their *Neil M. Gunn: A
Highland Life*, published in 1981.

Later on, maybe more than twenty years later than our first,
wartime letters, I would be trying to pull him across from Dingwall to
Inverness where our meetings were. I wanted to have a good talk
before I went on to the arguments and cross-talk of the Highland
Panel. It was more than letters; it was still a striking of minds, but I
think we always kissed. But can I now remember when we first wrote
to one another? With the help of the letters, I think I can.

I think we must have kept most of our letters to one another. His were
usually dated, mine seldom. For both of us there were family anxieties
and tragedies; we counted that the other would surely understand. I try
to remember back. In all the letters we kept – both of us – there was
always a background of the good and long-lasting relation that we had.

At first, when I reread the old letters, on copies by the National
Library, I thought these were the only ones to survive. One day I was

hunting for something else out of the past, and here were more letters hiding in the back of a drawer. Why had I not sent them to Edinburgh? I suppose because they were less about politics and more about one another, a kind of dance we were making, the finding of a relationship which went deeper than politics. Clearly I couldn't bear to let them go. They settled into the dark of memory.

We wrote as writer to writer, knowing that we needed feeding with praise, and our writings were so different that we were never jealous; we wanted to help. Most of the letters in the National Library are mainly about politics at a time when Scotland was deeply involved in working out what political action was really needed, and how to get it. These letters had become part of history, and history must be open, always be trying to show something, to teach, not just to hold hands, as a letter can do. Yet it would be wrong to think of Neil as a politician. He would achieve things through other ways.

These letters which I did not send to the National Library had, certainly, some politics of a kind, a wrestle, pulling and changing the one to whom the letter was sent. But mainly they were goldening an already good relation between writer and writer. We were getting to know one another or, perhaps, to know the picture which each author wanted the other to see. There was also a lively change of ideas and much more about our trade: writing. At that time I was making and writing poems and songs and in a way this was also politics. My books were seldom acceptable in the British or Anglo-American market – or whatever you choose to call your readers. The delight I got from Neil's liking and admiration of them was a lovely gift. I suppose it was so near the heart that I didn't want to let others see it. Now I can look more coldly and I shall let you into these letters as well. Neil would laugh and agree.

Remember that 1941 was a bad year for the Allies against Hitler's Germany. The battle of London and south England had begun and would get worse and worse from then on. Rommel was winning in north Africa. Food was difficult, though in May more was coming in from America, but it was still rations for all. At least I felt that my small farm had a genuine importance. By then my eldest son and his wife, both doctors in London, were having a hard time to get enough to eat, and when I could I sent them anything I could lay hands on. The younger ones had fairly adequate food at school, but I tried to produce a bit more in the holidays. Winter was a time of tatties and herring. Like the rest in the village I had salt herring and potatoes for too many meals. There were plenty of other problems, but at least I thought my small fields were worth the work I put into them. It comes into the letters here and there. I was proud of it. That was the year when Russia came in as our ally and we old Lefties made songs and stories about them. All this was the background of our letters.

Neil was working as hard as I was, though his problems were rather different. 'I've been in a spot of trouble,' he writes, 'what with flu and my brother in a critical condition following a motor crash. Even my typewriter has gone wrong on me. And my publishers have snowed me under with proofs of a simple country novel of over 200,000 words. Which length should be prohibited by law.'

He goes on to my suggesting that some of us in Scotland, interested in such matters, should keep in touch. 'I do agree. For many years now I have given most of my spare time to politics, behind the nationalist scenes mostly, and indeed over this broad northend there is no one with whom I talk literary or kindred affairs.'

He really enjoyed talking (for it was always much more like talk than letter-writing) about writing – at least when he liked it, as, I think, he liked most of mine. This was lovely for me, since he always picked up my rhythms and the feeling behind them. He told me about some of what he was doing, especially about a play which had been produced by a Yorkshire fishing community – I believe in their own particular dialect! 'When the son in the play had got one or two of his long speeches off his chest with mounting gusto, the local newsagent told me, "I had a quick look round to see how Campbell, the baker, was taking it." He added, "It's surely a new kind of play, yon."'

Then he goes on to making a short sketch of what the Russians are doing in small fishing communities by co-operation methods, more about drifters and 'the primordial urge a man has to do things for himself' and 'the just balance between society and the individual'.

Another long letter in March 1941 came in answer to what must have been a letter from me after I had been out with the ring-net boats. He says, 'I have never been at the ring-netting but the sea terms, from the wind that freshens to the herring that can be smelt, are the common tongue of fishermen. You get them so unobtrusively dead right!' That was indeed the kind of letter which set me up.

He goes on to a 'highbrowism' which I had complained about. But I think we had two rather different ideas of what highbrowism was. It didn't really matter. What did matter was the happiness I got from these long letters. The feeling that here was someone who understood what I was trying to do. There was a line or two about Proust and then about the traditional Gaelic stories. He adds:

> I haven't the Gaelic – only a few remembered words, for my father had it, but then I happened to be of the generation for whom Gaelic was supposed to be a drawback in life. We laughed at it as outlandish. Oh the propaganda was very subtle. God, what crimes have been committed in the name of propaganda. But it's not so easy as all that as I could show . . . To disentangle values here is interesting, and then to translate those values into our age . . . might be exciting, especially if a few swans began taking to wing.

This is an allusion to a story of mine, 'Five Men and a Swan'. I think he really enjoyed seeing my stories and poems which I was finding such difficulty in getting published. He wrote about some poems, 'There are penetrating things in it and a frankness clear and wise. The dross of self-assertiveness and self-pity and battles long ago is burned away and the ultimate spirit is seen, before our eyes – the new road.' Meantime he and I both had our publishing difficulties. But he always found a market for his short stories. Once he sold one to the *New Yorker*.

Another June letter is typed – a help and a slight standing back for me. It is a strange kind of pain to see the handwritten letters again, harder to disentangle oneself. He had just had a bad review from the *New Statesman* – a 'clever, liverish, superior lad'. He adds:

> I have read the novel reviews in the NS always with an irritation, a feeling of their vindictive waspishness. The only writer who knew this type well was D. H. Lawrence, for he showed how they live in their heads – and he knew their heads. Their reacting to a book like mine – and inevitably to much of your work – is pretty much like the reaction of a certain kind of homosexual to straight sex. Dealing at such length with such crude humans I particularly sinned in not making them brutal – and so satisfying the subtle sadism of the stickit intellectual. If I say as much it's not because

they have attacked me – they have not deigned to notice me so far – but because they have attacked good men with so utter a lack of a humanity, of the warmth in praise or denunciation, out of which life comes, that in some sensitive, really creative minds they must occasionally induce despair. I may be unfair to Antony in this, for I am really referring to a type I know . . .

He had some good reviews and wasn't complaining but he was shocked by the 'torrid negating' which seems to be wrong for a book (this must have been *The Silver Darlings*) and I am astonished that the *NS* didn't recognize it. However it does make occasional mistakes! Both the *Lit Supp* and the *Guardian* were enthusiastic. I myself had clearly been worried about the 'love part' but he defends it, saying simply, 'it was so' and he probably knew.

At the back of all these letters, was the war: how long, how long. And it was spreading across the world. Perhaps our letters to one another were partly to keep out the real news which had to be borne. We never mentioned it; we only kept to what was appropriate, as though we were writing a book about ourselves. Not that it seemed like that at the time. Only when I look back.

Our letters often came in spurts – something we had forgotten to say in the last one and it must be said! Sometimes he wrote about writing: in a letter in June 1941, for instance:

I'm merely trying to get at the difficulties of men who, as you say, read Annie S. Swan with eagerness. Now Annie as literature may be pretty poor stuff, but she does supply for them the romantic movement – the same as the surrealist lighthouses are after! They fill in her stuff with their own stark emotions. If you could provide the vehicle as surely as Annie, then we'd be back once more in the old ballad splendour. And then, by the Lord, we'd be going somewhere!

But he, himself, always seemed to like my own poems very well.

We seemed to be keeping up with one another's problems. I wrote to him about some very embarrassing things that had happened on the river, when people whom I liked and who, I think, liked me, were involved in what was no doubt their usual pleasure. But I couldn't let down my other friend – the keeper. So it was all rather a pity and, worse, an embarrassment (but probably for everyone). Later, I did a bit of poaching myself and realized how fascinating it was. It was nice having Neil hold my hand at a distance; we hadn't even met.

Neil, in the summer of 1941, was lent (not by me):

a batch of poetry books by modern fellows – Day Lewis, Auden, MacNeice, Ezra Pound. I have read 'em all, but find in me no particular desire to read 'em again. Day Lewis produces an interesting effect: thought and intellect are so busy compressing what he has to say into a richness that the total effect is just wordy. An awful nemesis of arid dryness can overtake the too agile intellect. MacNeice uses his words like a poet and has the poet's vision of a thing, but he seems to have nothing positive to say. I know that no doubt properly interprets the age. But does it really? In any case, does it justify the poet? You get the effect that all is baloney and each thing more inconsequent than the next . . .

No mention of Auden!
He goes on:

If I knew that they positively and affirmatively believed this or that, then I could get their point . . . When they have a sort of Leftish direction and a sort of belief in 'humanity', a sort of adolescence in philosophy and physical affairs, oh well, life is a bit short for too much of that. Now when it came to Lawrence [D.H.], his late poems, the metre is quite as modern, free and loose, but O Lord it penetrates, it pierces, it stings. Lawrence is on his feet with something to say.

In the same letter he talks of a 'curious experience'. He 'began stoically to read' the translation by Leishman of Rainer Maria Rilke – 'and oh sweet Heaven, never have I found the exhilaration of poetry like it these twenty years. How lovely, how supreme! I could not get over it for days! And when I thought that this was only a translation!' He went on for more and more praise, then to me about a photograph, then: 'As for nationalism being like a worm in front of a steam roller, I

disagree entirely. Men will get fed to the teeth with the steam roller.'
A first whisper of politics.

Sometimes he ends up his letters with odd bits: 'No, I was never engaged to a girl in Oban at all'. What had I been asking? 'But sure they shift about, and anyway if there's a lassie willing to pay me such a high compliment, how could I be after denying it? And if she jilted me, it was just tough on me. With blessings for the happy laugh your letter brought. We're off to Eigg on Friday for a fortnight.'

And a postscript: 'Rob Ruadh's Rolling Wave. What a grand name for a boat, bang in the old tradition, I have never come across it. Should I ever have the pleasure to meet Rob, we may have a small one on the heads of it.'

The next letters are all in the summer of 1941 and never a word about the war. Maybe that was very intentional. We had so much of it but never knew what was really happening. Perhaps it was best not to think too much about it. We wrote mostly about our books or poems. In one letter from him: 'About politics – we'll leave it mean time.' But it was always at the back. My own letters seemed to be asking for some kind of help. In one of my long letters to him we are in the middle of a discussion:

> I'm still not sure what you mean. You see, I don't think it's possible to make much of a life unless one is prepared to accept with goodwill and eagerness, some kind of discipline. It must be of a certain strictness or one won't feel it; it won't be anything solid, enough to give the sense of worthwhileness without which you'll want your dram. That, I think, is what we're after in Convention. It's what I'm after anyway. The whole end of man, the heart of the cyclone, you won't get there by just dithering around, nice as that may be on a fine day and the sweet smell coming off the heather. I think that the strong can impose this on themselves but the weak may have difficulty, may want something part willed and part imposed. That's what a political party should be able to give . . .
> Are you doing anything about the Convention fishing committee?
> . . . I've got a few facts about fishing in the USSR. But the difficulty here is that east coast and west coast are each out for themselves . . .

I wonder how much Neil was aware of some changes coming inexorably into the landscape of his dreams, the Highlands which were beginning to advertise themselves for the tourists. They came also, of course, from the men – and even the women – coming back from the outside world, and that world filtering in through newspapers, through radio and in the near future, telly. Even during the war it was clear that new voices were there to stay. For one thing, men must get used to women barging into their odd jobs and occupations and money-earning. It is all very well to think that the good old love-game was still the most important thing for the young, especially the girls. These same girls had taken over men's work in a very competent way, and, as part of the game, were beginning to expect more help around the house from the men. This went with female feelings about some totally man-organized bodies, such as the Church. By now women had shared, not only danger, but leadership.

What then, was the general political feeling we were moving into, when politics spread further than Scotland during the last war years? It was, of course, the politics of the Left and that, in the end, was communism in some form. In the late 1930s, just before the war, there had been considerable feeling in the Labour Party that the Left should join up. However, most of the big trade union votes were against it. This is all an old story, but I remember going as the elected representative of the Argyll Labour Party (such as it was at the time) and holding up my voting hand when sitting next to the many members representing one of the big unions, who glared at me. All these delights of Blackpool.

It was a happiness for me to find so much political agreement taken for granted between Neil and myself. Like everyone else, we were, to start with, totally pro-Russian. We should realize by now that, but for the swing round of the Soviet Union, Hitler would have won his war. I, by the way, was on Hitler's 'black list'. When I was told this, and it was a bit upsetting, one of my fishermen friends said, 'Ah, no bother, we'll take you across to Canada in one of the boats.'

It was also taken for granted by Neil, as soon as we got talking, that I was not only a Leftie but totally pro-Scotland as something apart from, though not an enemy of, 'the United Kingdom'. Also that I should be doing something about it, using whatever means existed for pushing our political ideas into reality. At that time, of course, the main way to get our ideas across was good old radio. He writes in October 1942:

> We should be able to use the BBC. But we can't in Scotland because London control is absolute. It would take me too long to tell you of the fights I have had over that programme. After sitting on the script for *six months* the BBC Glasgow wired me saying they had been offered thirty minutes by London and would I reduce my script by ten minutes. Even if I had been willing it would have been impossible, because of the varied amount of matter present, all balanced into a whole. But I was by no means willing, and began by telling them so. Glasgow was not to blame of course. So I have been writing London. And then London was directly responsible for a hitch at the beginning whereby the first minute and a half of the programme had to be cut, with the very worst effect in the broadcast's opening. It is really becoming a trifle painful.

I can't remember when or where I first actually met Neil to see and speak with. I suppose we felt we knew one another so well that we didn't need anything more. Was he what I expected? I don't know.

When he and I weren't talking politics in our letters, we were likely to talk as well about our own job: writing fiction. He agreed that he did on the whole write one good novel and then a rather less good one. He was, after all, writing for his living, and shoving little bits, beautifully written, but without much solidity, into any magazine which would pay even the small amount which most of them paid. Still and all, a cheque is a cheque. When we actually met, we talked, as all writers do, about publishers and their dark deeds, though we both got on reasonably well with our own.

But the main thing was always beyond that. It was our vision of how Scotland should go. This was before the idea of Europe as a whole had become possible. We were still nursing the wounds of the war years, the feeling that we were not being told what was happening, but occasionally finding some politicians who had really hit the nail on the head. One or the other of us might be going to Edinburgh to bite the heels of whatever politician or administrator we thought would actually do something. We both much liked the looks of Edinburgh. Glasgow hadn't yet sorted itself out into the kind of awareness of what a modern city should be, which it now seems to have. We were both very conscious of our tie to the Highlands and Islands as a special problem. I remember crossing to one of those far islands on an official visit in the early days of the Highland Panel and thinking: What would Neil want us to say and do? And the boat bouncing on big waves and all but the Fisheries officer and myself being sea-sick.

We found ourselves more and more on the political Left, no doubt the Loony Left from time to time, but who can always guess which is the right road? I was less suspicious of what was going on in the Soviet Empire than he was. We certainly believed a great deal of Stalin's big lie. But we also believed in the hidden true heart of the lie which sometimes let itself be apparent, and which is perhaps hiding again today, but with a better chance of becoming a reality.

Many of the keenest thinkers and writers among the young Scots had gone all the way to communism, whatever they called it. Neil writes to me, early on (but we started feeling for one another's politics almost at once) about the Left: 'There are a great number of us prepared to travel in that direction, and with such democratic history as we have behind us, it seems to me absurd – even from a Marxist point of view – that we should copy Russia. I, too, have fallen foul of my communist friends at this point.' And then : 'We have had enough ideological splitting of hairs in our own history, especially in religion – and the Russian business is pretty much on that level.'

I sometimes wish he had actually gone into politics, though I suppose he would have found it thin and full of holes. Instead he was put on to a commission of enquiry that was being set up by the Secretary of State – of all unlikely things, on post-war hospital co-ordination. All meetings were in Edinburgh, which meant three days away from home for Neil. Why didn't they put him on to the herring enquiry? Perhaps because they thought he knew too much about it and might have ideas that they didn't want.

I was still trying to run a farm with a minimum of the kind of modern machinery that takes the weight off one's human body. I had to develop skills which were totally useless later on. But there was a certain satisfaction in the more intimate relation with cows and sheep – and even, in the early years, the hand-sown oat seeds and hand-tied sheaves. And of course everything took longer, especially if it had to go to London to be okayed. There was very little publishing in

Scotland, though that was to come soon. Meantime there were constant small irritations. I think Neil had been entangled in some of them. Another thing which worried him was not feeling able to face cheerfully some of the things which he, more and more as he got an ever-widening audience, was asked to do or write. In one letter he says:

The thing that troubles me most of all is refusing the University boys when they ask me to stand for Lord Rector. Glasgow has done it twice, and Aberdeen, and Edinburgh, and now here is Edinburgh again. And once more I refuse. I hate refusing, because I would like to help the lads, but this public stuff is just not for me. But it is difficult rigging up excuses. I try to square my conscience by saying that I do my fair share of public work one way or another. And perhaps I do – don't you think? Or am I trying to drag you in to soothe my conscience also? Blast it, anyway.

I expect I was a bit unsympathetic about that, having had, myself, to learn the hard thing of being a parliamentary candidate's wife, and, later, wife of a hard-working MP! That letter of Neil's goes on to say he thinks I'm doing well 'in the fields and with the folk. I suppose it was the way old Grundtvig in Denmark went about setting up the whole Danish economy, based on nationalism, the traditions of the folk. And begod he did pretty well!' I think now that Neil was feeling that some of the wilder things he had been involved with, had not done much good to the cause of Scotland as a whole.

The next new letter I have was a long one, written in the summer of 1943 and 'these days are so lovely anyhow that the thought of work fair goes agin me' but he is hopeful about the film of *The Silver Darlings*.

Nothing definite yet about beginning, but then they live on telegrams. The BBC have asked me to do a fisherman Portrait – a 45 min affair – and I've just been putting them off by telephone – until later in the year . . . I liked your remarks about discipline and not dithering in a recent letter, but I could do with a lot more of the dithering myself. And I must say, besides, that talk of discipline and all that comes very well from you! If I have a fellow in a novel who may have any sense of discipline at all, you sicken at the sight of him as a galahad. And accuse me of 'purity' and what not. So where are you? You'll have discipline just where and when you want it, and that is generally in some idealist affair, disguised under the name of practical politics. Fine day!

This is about half a page in which he is scolding me, and I can't remember at all what I had said to set him off. I must have annoyed him quite a bit to get him writing that. Sorry, Neil! Anyway he was giving me a good scolding, but it ends: 'I'm afraid I'm having a chuckle as I write this, but a chuckle sounds dreadfully heavy on a typewriter, so I had better stop this and go on to your eloquence about my joining Convention.'

Well, I'm not joining yet, not joining anything for a while. And you must give me credit for many long years of consistent service. I was at the beginning of the National Party, and years afterwards fought the Scottish Party in its beginnings and duly absorbed them. Just before the Convention break with the SNP I had got some Edinburgh folk to come into the SNP and they are now among its best workers. They don't want me, they say, to 'desert' them. And in Inverness – and so on. And the students of the University SNP Associations keep on asking me to be an Hon President. Now I'm not putting much stress on all that. I know what it's worth. But I do feel that for a little while yet I should go on working for the common cause, and sometimes be able to use what little influence I have in bringing about a natural healthy cohesion. Please give me a little time. And I can work all round, even if you think that's a somewhat self-important statement. For instance, here's a copy of John MacCormick's pamphlet on Convention. In sending it to me Dr Macdonald hopes that I'll be able to make it the subject of a full article in the *Daily Record*. Well, that's somewhat naïve! For how can I in the capitalist anti-nationalist press boost a pamphlet written to further the aims of a nationalist group? But I will try. I'll certainly write that article – and in such a way that they will have to hesitate before daring to refuse it. It will seem from the article that I'm giving Convention my blessing.

Neil goes on in the same long letter to become more himself, as if we were lying on the grass of the same meadow:

And you making me write all this on a day of such sunshine that it's off after the dead Philosopher I am, fair on to the moors, where there's a lost burn, where whiles I fish, and other whiles dip in a pool and sit on a rock to dry. By God, it's good. Peewits, grouse, and the individualism that takes the wandering air on its skin. I never enter that world but I can look back on other worlds with a certain eye; and if such a picture raises no more than a troubled pity in your attractive eyes, well, that's not an unattractive picture either. Or is it a conception too simple and pure – having a couple of worlds to make the best of? Hesitancies are meaningless and nothing definite and the hours going on – how exasperated a whole afternoon of it would make you! Yes? Life is earnest, life is simple – or how do the poet's words go, for I never could remember them? (He was an American of course) . . . I'm probably getting a little incoherent. They recently published *Highland River* in a 2/- edition, 25,000 of them – all gone. Also a new 7/6 edition – sold out. Such appalling luck for a poor Scots writer in Scotland. Are things already beginning to look up for us? Another smile all to yourself.

Surely, surely we'd smiled at one another, felt the same grass under our feet? But when? Hard that memory gets so dodgy as one gets old.

But so it went. And it was very difficult to get the various Scots politicians of the future to agree. Those were the worried days when we wrote to one another, about how best to do things, how to get going what seemed to us vital for Scotland. Perhaps those who read his books now will understand what we were after, how we tried to see what was happening, to picture the changes that were going on both in individuals and in society, perhaps to set new ideas going.

The press was slightly more friendly. The *Daily Record* on Scottish affairs agreed to a fortnightly article from Neil. This meant he had to be a bit less militant and must go into more agreement with Tom Johnston's ideas, a good thing in the long run though he felt a bit tied down at the time. Meanwhile meetings went on. I doubt if he ever made a real public speech. He wanted to explain things quietly, as one does on paper, not to shout about them. I was more of a shouter. Also

he realized how important the films had become and, in late 1942, he
was

> just on the point of signing an agreement for the filming of *The
> Silver Darlings* in the Highlands. The producer would be a Czech of
> international reputation in the film world and the scenario writer a
> Glasgow man. The idea is to do the whole thing on the spot with
> local talent – somewhat after *The Man of Arran* film.

What a marvellous film that would have been, with Karl Grune as
producer! But it never came off.

About then, he and I were thinking of writing a combined book on
the fisheries problem, but the difficulties would be immense and if it
were to be really good, it would involve a lot of travelling and
gathering of information. We were already thinking about post-war
constructive ideas. I quote: 'If nothing is done immediately after the
war – when the opportunity for many reasons (full fishing banks, few
boats, great demand, etc) would be perfect – then the whole industry
will go to the devil, as it did after the last war.' We were fully
conscious of the real world, although, as we did not realize until
afterwards, the civilian population of the UK was still getting very
little real news and hardly anything about the tremendous battles far
from Europe. Civilians only heard what the authorities thought was
good for them. Some of the things we most dreaded have in fact
happened in the Scottish fisheries industry.

He goes on:

> We have had enough blood for our life-times. At least that's the
> way I feel. But then I have always been a little repelled by the
> materialist interpretation of history and all the rest when it
> becomes the new religion. Religion and ideals and what-not. Fine!
> But oh God, they do manage to prosecute them to the nth in
> cruelty. A drunk man with a revolver is a happy child compared
> with the fellow who has power to convert you. Anyway, if history is
> to have any meaning at all, surely hundreds of years of understand-
> ing of the democratic concept as we have had it in Scotland must
> count for something. If not – then don't expect us to be impressed.
> After all, take the organization of the Scottish Church, from Kirk

session or local soviet up to the General Assembly and you might say it gave Russia its governmental pattern. What a wealth of belief and enthusiasm and shedding of blood went to that foundation! And what do you enlightened revolutionaries think and say of it today? At least we have something to go on. Which is my whole case for Scotland. I know what you mean, it's no good just altering things so that folk can go twice a week to the films instead of once. But that's precisely what they'll do however you alter things. What could be altered for the better is the community spirit and the kind of flicks. Though here again I am not sure that the highbrows should have it their own way.'

Clearly by now he and I were talking, in our long letters, about basic political ideas, which is why they are still relevant. But also we were encouraging one another in how to live a reasonable life, with some idea of the future. He and his brother were thinking about buying a new boat when the war was over: 'hellsbells this bloody war'. And good advice to me on disguising my feelings, especially in poems.

I kept almost all his letters. He kept some of mine, but, luckily, not all. Sometimes I poured out my worries and uncertainties on to him, most of all when, as often happened, I did something which went against local ideas of what the lady of the 'Big House' should be saying or doing. I could never allow myself to understand how much of a gap there really was between myself and them, yes, all of them. I loved Carradale, but not in the way the people of Carradale wanted or – most of them – understood. It was partly a gap of some kinds of experience: of other countries and other centuries, and other ambitions. The gap hurt. I tried to dodge it. Neil saw what was happening and gave me good advice, and comfort as well, sometimes.

Up until the 1950s the whole of Great Britain was still crawling out from the war years. Still no going into shops and getting whatever you wanted. We in Carradale watched eagerly as the big poles and wires went up and we could at last get electricity based on Highland water power, with all it meant for comfort and ease of working in the house, as well as some things like streetlights, which did not always please the local lads. There had also been the terrible post-war shock of the 'influenza', whatever it was, that killed so many of our men and women who had survived the fighting. But now we were getting the benefit of the scientific and medical knowledge that had shot into life after, and sometimes because of, the war. But one still couldn't buy new shoes for growing children, spare parts for machinery, or new crockery for table or kitchen.

There were deeper changes going on, a whole turnover and contradiction of a pattern which had somehow still survived, not least in Scotland. The pattern of master and servant, employer and employee, not quite the same as buyer and seller, but using many of the same concepts. Under our eyes this change was nibbling at our arts, whether in writing or painting – and by then the 'Glasgow School' had started, attaching colours and shapes in a new way. Accepted patterns of society are always behind the reality – and often shocked by it. The Scottish patterns, and above all the Highland one, might appear to be static, but all was change, even if an old wording survived. The clan chief might still exist nominally and those so minded accepted it on both sides, especially if they saw something in it for themselves – usually to do with the tourist industry.

The countryside changes were perhaps more delicate and because of that fascinating to writers, especially for those who had been very conscious of some class aspects, like Neil himself. He had appreciated the old class angers and attitudes; they made good patterns for stories, most of all when they were changing between generations. Yet there were even more remarkable changes in the attitudes and patterns of behaviour between men and women, boys and girls. This meant there was always grist for the author's mill. (And how many of today's readers have seen or smelt grist or taken their own corn to the real mill? I have, during the war, but only just. The same, I am sure, for Neil.) Odd, how some words survive.

You will find a strong awareness of the changes, not only in Neil's main novels, but even more clearly in the short stories that he obviously enjoyed throwing off. Many were based on the new possibilities which allowed him to make new patterns. In the Highlands the changes were often half covered by the old wordings and surface politeness. Neil would tease me for living in the Tigh Mor, the Big House, and he was fascinated and affectionate about my stumbles and worries and my political hopes for the classless society, which he and many others hoped to see.

He could explain how the people who hurt me really meant well. We wondered, when we met, whether this kind of thing had gone in the Soviet Union, and if so – but after that we found ourselves stuck. We both felt, as a great many others did, that communism was a good thing. And so it could be if it was run by saintly people who yet understood modern practical science including economics and eschewed power. But under what hedge to find them? So much was talked about but totally never put into action. Our political discussions drifted off into stories and the people and circumstances which we were inventing. We kept on having ideas about all this and from time to time we heard of something that fitted in, good or, more often, bad: 'Yes,' he writes to me, 'the landlord on the Inverness side of Kinlochleven did not like the idea of industry approaching his lonely sporting estate, so he either refused downright or named so high a figure that building homes for the workers on the sunny side was verboten.'

We tried to make sensible suggestions, for instance, about legal changes. And we kept on arguing and half agreeing about politics. From time to time I would send him one of my poems. In one letter back: 'Verily a capital and most wicked poem! When you ask me if you are talking through your hat – I just remember the hat. Any talk through it would be fascinating.' And so our dance went on happily twirling. We were both on the look-out for new Scots writers. He was delighted when he found something good – for instance Drinan's *Men of the Rocks* – and wrote excitedly to me about it. But never again about Auden (though I myself thought that he wrote fewer really good poems after 1943). For a time he shook off direct politics, and also his interest in industrial happenings in Scotland. In 1943 he writes: 'I have been completely out of touch of developments in the fishing industry since the war started. My car is laid up. I can't travel. An awful nuisance. But I hate writing about anything without first-hand contact somewhere.' And then: 'Trawling lands a vast quantity of fish compared with inshore fishing. There's the Herring Committee sitting, I should like to see its recommendations.' And on top of that there seemed to be a new possibility about a film.

An English writer told him 'that my country characters are far too sensitive and complex to be real. There may be a sense in which he is right if I can only catch it.' This worries him and he asks if I can help. I wonder what I wrote back. Meanwhile his typewriter had 'gone bust' and what can be more annoying? The next typed letter comes in 1944 and he is supporting 'the electric scheme', that is the water-power works which did mean reasonably cheap electric power to Scotland – though not, of course, enough to save us from nuclear power a historically few years on.

We were both supporting this kind of getting ahead, even if it might 'spoil the Highlands'. There was a lot of heart-burning about this, views – as well as houses, forest and cropland – destroyed, but that had to be. Yet, on the other hand, it was not sufficiently revolutionary. This brings him back into politics:

> The trouble with my communist friends is that they can't see that any sort of revolution necessary for this country should not be of the Russian kind in its execution or practice. We have freedom of expression about political personalities and affairs. Why not let us keep it? Well, surely we are civilized enough to carry through a new dispensation without first handing our liberty to the kind of folk which a mass movement shoves into power . . . I am really interested in your attitude to the C. Party. Folk like us had better take a stand somewhere.

Not that the letters were all about solid politics. Some of them were just advice and comfort to me in my problems and mistakes in Carradale. He writes:

> Complicated personal relations are the devil at any time, but when social, class etc relations are added, the old Cretan maze has nothing on 'em. Being as you fondly believe . . . a classless human, you may forget from your point of vantage how subconscious social elements do their work in eager hearts . . . Come off it a bit and smile. But never give in by an inch.

By that time I had been elected to the Argyll County Council, and a new set of friends and enemies.

The next letter is in 1946. And he has his new book 'with a landlord! – and a good one' (*The Drinking Well*). Neil will be much criticized for that, but it is what happens in the book. When one's characters decide, what can one do?

How easy to arrange for young fellows forming a kind of glen soviet and all that kind of sweet unreality! But I'm afraid, Naomi, whatever my writing may look like, I'm just a hard-bitten realist . . . Peace and constructiveness be with you, on the County Council and in your writing, now and ever more. I gather from a painter who was up here that the poets and literary highbrows of Glasgow look upon me as one who might have done something in literature if I hadn't turned my back to follow the primrose path of success! *The Green Isle* rather shook some of my communist friends (think of my introducing GOD), but now, trafficking with a landlord in order to find a way out of defeatism! Sure and it will be the finish of me . . . Never mind, it is a good old fight . . . And if they get obstreperous I might even do a psychoanalytic novel on coteries . . . But there's so little time for that.

By now I think he is getting tired, thinking too much of how little time was left. I know that feeling only too well. Yet the contracts were still coming in, and odd things were happening. For instance, a German prisoner of war was translating *The Green Isle* behind the barbed wire.

His next letter was about this *Green Isle of the Great Deep*, the most likely of his books to stand the test of time and go on being fascinating for anyone thinking about the morals of politics. He writes:

'How delightful of you to utter the ultimate compliment by saying you think *The Green Isle* was written for you. That sort of living response would make anyone write a book. In fact, I wrote *The Green Isle* right off, just because an old friend of mine in Ireland, who has mostly for company now his little grandson, was so affected by what he considered the inner truth of *Young Art* that he said I mustn't leave them at the River. So I didn't. Can you think of any better reason for writing a book?'

Whether it was or not, I feel in my bones that I had something to do with it! I wouldn't wonder if the tale of the old friend in Ireland was just thought up and embellished for a tease. He writes me a lovely letter about my book *The Bull Calves*. In fact, he sounds as if things were going nicely for him. The next letter was a year later and he was worried about buying the new house.

But then he has moved house and is giving me advice – especially about the Argyll County Council and about dealing with the Forestry Commission. But in all the letters he went back to *The Green Isle* and what it was about, and about different Highlandnesses, official and not, about the breaking up of old tribalisms and how to keep our heads in a time of whirling political changes. And then: 'Yes, I noticed Clause 5(c) of the Herring Bill.' After that about possible publishing in Glasgow. Things were going very fast for both of us and no doubt we, like many others, hoped for too much from the first Labour government in London.

By this time I was coming up to Inverness quite often, to meetings of the Highland Panel; I tried to see him if possible and, against my principles, fed him whisky. The evening I remember best was when the panel meeting was rather unexpectedly called for Hallowe'en – incidentally my birthday. Hallowe'en meant little to the Scottish Office, but I wasn't going to let this pass and I had brought trousers and a boy's coat with me as well as a good solid mask. After the meeting and a decorous supper, I dressed up and chased around some of the advisers from the Scottish Office who were staying at the more expensive hotel. I was thrown out, stiff with laughing, by the hotel porter, saying, 'We don't want any more boys here!' Still a bit mad, I ambled down to where the cars had been left. All but one was empty: in that one was Neil, perhaps having a bit of sleeping off. Fine! I opened the door, he didn't know who it was until I took off my mask and then we were happily in one another's arms. It made that Highland Panel meeting for me. Apart from anything else, I got a bit of new light on one of our fishery problems, and was able to discuss it with the panel the next day.

I think Neil saw through into what was actually happening in the Soviet Union before I did. But, indeed, all that is well discussed in Hart and Pick's book. I remember it differently – not unnaturally considering the years that have passed since then, and every year slightly altering one's memory of the years before. What I remember most is that we thought great political changes were about to be made.

In a sense we were right, but the froth at the top may not make the taste below any different. Writers are always twisting the real world into a suitable pattern for their own weaving. Which is why one should never believe them, however attractive one may find them. Neil and I certainly teased one another, though he was the worst tease, or at least he enjoyed it more than I did. To have one's teases taken seriously, one must be able to look down a bit; no doubt in the real inside of it the man is on top of the woman, whoever they might be in dull daylight. I am sure that didn't mean he could be unkind or unheeding of the females, and he realized that even a woman can have, not only good ideas, but – occasionally no doubt – the possibility of having them accepted by the wide world. But to give them power? Well, they can have power of a kind and it may work very well. But, after the war, in the 1950s and 1960s, women were walking away from that. They managed to become top dogs without becoming bitches. I'm not sure that Neil really held with that.

However it didn't affect us that much. Often we wrote – both of us I think – to tease, or to assist in a turn with a teasing smile, which is rather different. I'm sure Daisy must have laughed about my letters, especially the most 'feminist' of them, for I was often worried about his female characters, except of course the great breed of Highland mothers holding the fort. I admired them – and met a few in the flesh as well – but they were dying out in real life.

From time to time I bit Neil about this, usually when I had been bitten myself by the local respectables, who have more power in villages than in towns. In one letter from the 1950s I say: 'I am getting sick of these bloody narrow respectable Highlanders. No good will come to the country till it stops being so bloody respectable and the small amount of furtive fornication that goes on is no use at all.' I was feeling very fed-up at the time, with my neighbours 'titivating themselves up for the Mod'. Then 'as part of a job I went to see some crofts further north . . . the most beautiful country in the world' but 'they have all the vices of all peasants; the lies they told about these wretched boarded-out kids from Glasgow! . . . they will always do the easiest thing for the moment, even when they half see it's all wrong.' This was a committee set up to find what was happening to boarded-out children, mostly from Glasgow.

But we came back to books.

I found *The Other Landscape* waiting for me: fascinating. I read it last night. The main electricity gone, owing to a storm, and it isn't really a book to read by one candle! How good you are on certain states of mind . . . I wonder if the Highlands *are* really like this, the various skins of the onion, and something real underneath.

And now I do remember our first meeting, and how can I ever have forgotten it? It comes into my wartime diary, in February 1943, when we were getting the Convention started. There it is, the first time we touched one another, yes, getting off a tram, going to the Convention meeting, but coming out into the black-out and one another's arms.

Wednesday–Friday 24–26 February 1943
. . . Well then, meeting Neil Gunn in Glasgow, a tall, loose-limbed chap with grand bones, a kind of half squint, might have been Irish, might have been a fisherman, a bit like Willie Galbraith but with sense and ability. But probably as lazy – and maybe as fond of a glass, though he would take it with discretion. In no time at all we were walking hand in hand, laughing, he lifted me from a moving tram and kept his arms round me for that much longer than he need have. We talked mostly about Convention, the Beveridge report, committees, fishing, the film of his book, Alba our mother and the signs of the times. Yet there was an undercurrent through it all; he was saying he was going to the films that evening to see something special, but he came to the meeting. Yet, as we were going into the Usher Hall and the dusk on Edinburgh and the amethyst shadow deepening below the castle, he said, 'Why are you going to this meeting?' And I couldn't think at all, but I went. And when I got to the small room at the back where the other speakers were, and feeling nervous enough, there was Betty Mackenzie and by her a lad in battledress and it was a moment before I saw it was Stewart Watson, come up from Berwick on twelve hours' leave, and then I knew why I had come.

We trooped on to the platform, and everyone else seemed easy and confident except myself – and perhaps John MacCormick. Lady Glen Coats [member of Liberal Party] was being very much a practised speaker, and the minister of course wouldn't worry. I felt half sick . . .

I was on fourth, after the collection and Lady G.C. who was pretty awful. There were about five hundred there, though the papers next day said more. It was an elderly audience mostly but I kept looking towards Neil. John made a good speech but didn't explain enough about what Convention is. The minister was really talking about the Church and I felt rubbed up the wrong way. I shoved the mikes away and pitched my voice low, for I know I could carry to the back of this hall. I began to talk about ordinary people, and I think I spoke well and with passion and poetry, because I felt two or three times that tension in the audience, and I felt like a chewed rag at the end myself, and then we had 'God save' and 'Scots wha hae' backed by the organs. Then I was talking to the Rendels and Uncle Willie and plenty more and Stewart looking at me with soft Highland eyes, and I kissed him. He had to get a train, but said would I send him papers.

Well then, most of the Convention folk went into the Rutland Hotel and everyone had drinks excepting myself, and Uncle Willie had gone back, so I said to Neil will you see me back – there had been a suggestion that William Power would come too, but I said Neil had better come back for him, and indeed Neil knew well enough that I was on for some devilment and away with us into the black-out and one another's arms, and I feeling all the time as though we were coming back from a Carradale dance and this Highlander the same as any of the rest of them. And the great pleasure we had to be kissing one another in the respectable midst of Edinburgh, and speaking of poaching and the companionship under the stars, and the fortunate thing that I had come back to Scotland!

THE ELEMENTAL IN NEIL GUNN

THE ELEMENTAL
IN NEIL GUNN

George Bruce

I FIRST MET Neil Gunn in the early 1940s in inauspicious
circumstances. Somewhat worn out after a day's teaching at
Dundee High School for Boys I dropped into a compartment of the
train which took me over the Tay Bridge to my home in Wormit. I
greeted one of the two other occupants, J.B. Salmond, the editor of
the *Scots Magazine*, who had published a few of my poems in it. He
introduced me to Neil Gunn. I can recollect nothing of the
conversation, but I know it was tentative and unenthusiastic though
I remember vividly the features and presence of the novelist.
Many years after Neil Gunn told me, 'I thought you were a
dried-up intellectual.' The fact was that so far from having any
feeling of superiority, as the phrase might imply, I was struck almost
dumb by meeting the man who had written the opening pages of
Morning Tide. There was a particular reason for my mind focusing on
these pages, and not simply on account of their merit. In what they
did they contradicted my conviction of the direction in which the
novel of the future must go.

Surprising as was the new direction and impetus which Mac-
Diarmid had given to poetry by the end of the 1920s, the
achievement was evidently a departure from traditional Scottish
poetry. The popular novel had degenerated into the stuffiness and
materialism of Hugh Walpole and the later Arnold Bennett. But
F.R. Leavis's pamphlet, *Mass Civilization and Minority Culture*, took

it for granted that if a new novel was popular it could not be good literature. So the intense, subjective literary visions of Virginia Woolf, which I found absorbing, were appropriate and necessary achievements. Similarly in poetry Eliot's great poem on the contemporary decivilization, *The Waste Land*, demanded of the would-be poet there should be no flight into the country idealism of the weekend poets who were to be found between the covers of *Poems of Today*. Consequently when I picked off the shelves of recent acquisitions in King's College Library at Aberdeen University *Morning Tide* by Neil Miller Gunn, while the title attracted me on account of my origins, I was on guard against any romantic trap, but within a page my guard was down, and I was reading and rereading the passages of the ebb. I had to tell someone. I found John Speirs, who by this time was taking his second degree in Cambridge, and was a student, friend and admirer of F.R. Leavis. I waited outside the library for some time for his qualified verdict, such as might be expected of one whose distinction as literary critic has been acknowledged. I remember the place, the time, some fifty-eight years ago, and the exact words: 'It's not possible.'

The surprise of this critic was due first to the directness, power and vividness of the words, but also to the discovery of a continuity of values and perceptions which seemed no longer available in England. The shock of discovery in *Morning Tide*, after the enjoyment of its immediate impact, was in the sense of the experience belonging to us all, returning us to a source of life not far distant even in the physical sense to anyone who lived in Scotland. In Gunn's case the sea had been the provider – and destroyer – for generations. In an essay Gunn comes to the sea after describing the scenery of Caithness and Sutherland, but in the art form of the novel where the pursuit is of a whole the circle is completed, the source includes the end, sometimes even in a single image. In his poem *The Spanish Trilogy* Rainer Maria Rilke, whom Neil Gunn greatly admired, wrote:

Out of this cloud see: that so wildly
Covers the star that just now was – (and out of me)
Out of that hilly country yonder which night

And night wind has for a time – (and out of me)
Out of this river in the glen which catches
The light of a torn sky – clearing – (and out of me),
Out of me and all those to make one single thing, Lord.

(Translation: Ruth Speirs.)

Throughout the poem the invocation 'To make *one* thing' is repeated, but to Gunn the single thing, that which includes the elemental and the personal, is given; given as integrity was given to the uncomprehending child, but apprehended by the writer in response to a happening in a particular place in Scotland. But it immediately becomes human experience, so that Professor Tokasaburo Nakamura in Japan will see the location as like his own country and certain characters in the novels as recognizable in Japanese terms.

Initially what is given to the novelist is the sound, movement, character and content of speech, and this reaches the pages of Neil Gunn in dispute or tale-telling or simply domestic conversation naturally and convincingly. The problem of the modern novel is the absence of a social rhetoric whereby the dignity or intensity of life can be recorded within a large context. A formal expression is required which can rise out of the conversational level, and this is not something which can be manufactured by a writer in isolation. This too requires to be given. With this in mind, despite its frequent quotation, one must listen again to the passage about the boy on 'the curving beach' where 'the tide was at low ebb and the sea quiet except for a restless seeking among the dark boulders.'

> Below the high-tidal sweep of tangleweed the beach sloped in clean grey-blue stones rounded and smooth, some no bigger than his fist, but some larger than his head. As he stepped on them they slithered and rolled with a sea noise. The noise rose up and roared upon the dusk like a wave. All around no life was to be seen, there was no movement but the sea's.

Here is a small human warmth, momentarily alive, measured against the effects of the element, the sea, on stones that have had their being through geological time. The size of the person may be diminished in the desolation with its vague threats of violence and non-human power, but in bringing the boy intimate with the stones – 'some no bigger than his fist, but some larger than his head' – close as his breathing to the reader, the marvel of being transcends all other considerations. One follows the practical things he does on the beach, gathering bait for his father's fishing, at the level of concern of Hugh, but no higher, and at the same time sees him in the context of imponderable vastnesses.

This is the immediate impression of the recording of an event that happened, transposed into an episode in a novel. The whole event includes the sensation of the place and time as these were experienced by the boy. The event presses for expression. This was the extent of Neil Gunn's intention. When he reread what he had written later he discovered an additional level of experience, which he related to me in a recorded interview in 1970:

> An odd thing happened years after the book had been published: the whole scene in the ebb gathered a symbolism which hadn't struck me when writing it. I saw life coming from the sea, then slipping back and coming again over perhaps a million years until at last it reached the dry land.

A few months after Neil Gunn's death in 1973 Heinrich Böll came to Scotland as the first holder of the Scottish Arts Council's Neil Gunn International Fellowship. The idea of the fellowship had pleased Neil Gunn greatly when he had been informed of it in the autumn of 1972. He was also taken by Böll as the first appointment, though he never met him, and was simply dependent on my description of the character of the novelist, who won a Nobel Prize for literature. I recorded an interview with Heinrich Böll. On the subject of symbolism, after I had suggested that the burning of an army jeep in his novel *End of a Mission* was a symbolic act, his reply might have come from Neil Gunn. Laughing, he said, 'It's not meant to be symbolic – no – it's both, you know, it's reality and symbolic.' Later he added, 'I want to show that symbol and reality are one.'

Seventeen years after *Morning Tide* Gunn is evidently immediately conscious of the symbolism as in *The Silver Bough*, where Grant, the archaeologist, is the central character. 'Grant stood looking from the little window as from a newer kind of earth house . . . For a miraculous moment the cat appeared on the garden wall. A blackbird whistled and was gone. Between the bursts he heard the pounding thunder of the sea.' And later when 'Old Fachie' sends his dog to round up a cow among the young corn. 'There were no other figures to be seen and in a moment the little drama with the old bent figure might of been of any Age back to Neolithic times.' Still the miracle is in the actual events and these are bound together by the presence of the elements. The strength of the presence is all-important. In *Morning Tide*, in the ebb another comes on the scene:

> The dark undulating water rose from him to a horizon so far away that it was vague and lost. What a size it was! It could heave up and drown the whole world . . . He glimpsed the rushing waters as a turbulent whiteness released out of thunderous sluices . . . A short distance away, right on the sea's edge, he saw one of the boulders move. His heart came into his throat. Yet half his mind knew that it could only be some other lonely human in the ebb. And presently he saw the back bob up for a moment again.

The fisherman is also looking for bait: 'Seeking among the boulders there like some queer animal! . . . There was no one else . . . It was as though they shared this gloomy shore, beyond the world's rim, between them. There was a secret importance in it.'

The perception is born of the man himself – the boy who had been taken to sea by his father at age ten, who by age eleven had helped with the planting of potatoes for the family, and had gone to the hill to help with the cutting and drying and stacking of peat on the peat hag. Significantly, after he had resigned from his post in the Customs and Excise to become a full-time writer, he sold his house, and bought a boat, which led to a holiday trip, the crew being himself, his wife Daisy, and for a time his brother John. The literary outcome was to be a light-hearted account, *Off in a Boat*. This tone is set by the title of the first chapter, 'How Not to Buy a Boat', and a deal of good-humoured badinage spreads throughout the book, but the character of the element itself, the character of the landscape with its thin spread of small dwellings as seen from the sea, and the personal history of the writer, make divorce between this presumed escape from commitment to the truth of fiction impossible:

Across the sea loch beyond our boat, little settlements or townships were scattered here and there, and individual dwellings; and in the vast treeless area that the eye covered everything was static, so that each house looked wind-swept and very quiet, while the landscape itself took on a dream quality that had in its stillness something incommunicably sad. As we sailed round the wild north-west coast, this effect had been particularly strong. It is an effect, no doubt, entirely in the mind of the beholder, but surely there is, too, that extra-universal feeling of the essential loneliness of human life and even something of the mystery of its being and doing on a planet of so remote and incredible a geological past. For looking thus on Skye we did, in truth, get the effect of looking on a planet, on one small curve of the green hide that formed over the forming structure of the earth. And to feel as much does not lessen the sweetness of wind and sun on the face, or the pleasure of seeing the plant life or watching the birds.

This is the cosmological vision implied, and sometimes explicit, in novel after novel. In terms of time and size man is diminished to nothing, which logically might lead to the concept of the meaninglessness of the universe, but here in this vision there are factors which give a dignity to human life which cannot be affronted by chronological time. There is the strange place that is made for the view – an 'extra-universal feeling' and then in the scene itself 'everything was static'. The perspective is repeated, I believe, in all the novels involving tragedy or suffering. In *The Serpent*, Tom the Philosopher – so named wryly – ascends a hill, reflecting on changes in his lifetime in the village:

> Yet it still was attached to the soil, a crofting hamlet, and as he looked the Philosopher saw figures singling their turnips in between the green cornfields on the narrow cultivated lands behind the houses. With their slightly bent heads they moved so slowly that it was easy to get the illusion of an inner meaning or design that never changed.

Illusion is the appropriate word for the sceptical 'Philosopher' to use, but when from the turmoil of life the perception of the human being is given special meaning by such terms of reference, one concludes that this is a device whereby interior patterns are discovered. Tom has been responsible for the death of his father. Stricken with guilt he takes to the hills, where his mother pursues him:

> Now she leaned with a hand against a boulder, stooping slightly like one drawing harsh laboured breaths. Then on again; but the ground was broken and her exhaustion must have been very great, for, when she stumbled and fell, she drooped in upon herself like one of the boulders, and, listening acutely, he heard the dry whining of her distress.

The reader is to see the mother as 'like one of the boulders'. She is placed among an effect of the elements, but like Hugh in *Morning Tide* in another place of boulders, as his humanity is gathered into 'boy', hers is discovered as 'mother'.

> But while he was yet a little way off, she got to her feet to continue her journey towards the horizon she had set before her. As he drew in behind her on her right side, she became familiar to him as his mother, in her body and its movements and its laboured breath. The familiarity touched him sharply and in order not to startle her too much he called from twenty yards: 'Mother!'

Surely this is part of one of the great passages of literature in English. It culminates in the recognition of motherhood, the journey towards which takes her through a world of stone, in which she journeys 'towards the horizon'. The sensation of the discovery of humanity is intensified by the phrase 'But while he was yet a little way off', echoing the expression of recognition of the son by the father in the parable of the Prodigal Son, 'But when he was yet a great way off'. Unceasingly, the elemental made its statements to the consciousness of Neil Gunn. The achievement is the finding of adequate expression. Earlier I referred to the lack of a social rhetoric making appropriate expression of moments of crisis so that these are contained. Yet the solution was given to Neil Gunn, whether or not he consciously saw it, given him with the insecurity of the sea and the security of family life. The application of the Authorized Version of the Bible in the passage quoted is specific, and something of its economy and rhythm is present at the end of *Morning Tide*:

> There is great beauty in the truth. It comforts the breast, and the heart rejoices in its knowledge of the abiding things that are as the features of truth's face. The wind and the rivers, labour, the sea and the sun. The eye has seen them, and the ear heard, and they are known of the body and of the hands. Even now as in the immemorial ages. Nor is the eye ever satisfied with seeing, nor yet the ear with hearing.

But for the dramatic purpose this might be regarded as pastiche. The reader, however, is inside the mind of Kirsty, who has been reading from Ecclesiastes to her mother, and we are told, 'Kirsty's voice was the voice of legend. It penetrated the years, going back into far time . . . ' It leads to the symbolism of Kirsty washing Hugh's feet. Nevertheless outwith the biblical ambience, when Hugh, now knowing his mother is not going to die, decides to leave the house, the style of the narrative is consonant with the preceding passages:

> Nor could the closed house hold him. The front door was unlocked. Round by the gable corner he paused and looked on the world. The fields, the crofts, every known thing, asleep in the grey of the dawn that was turning to silver and brightness. The sea glittered, and even as he looked, away north-east, the red rim of the sun pushed itself slowly up beyond the horizon. Soon the water between threw off flakes of vivid colour as big as moons.

Time was when such a passage might be categorized as 'purple prose', but it is in the context of the boy's perception, no doubt, as Neil Gunn as boy and man had seen it. There are certain influences that cannot be quantified. The boy, Hugh or Neil, had not set out to see a sunrise. The experience was unavoidable, and once allowed to possess the mind, what was received on the retina remains awaiting recall by the writer, when circumstances require its verbal expression.

Near the end of his life I stood with Neil Gunn on the grassy platform in front of his home that looks down on the Beauly Firth, and talked with him as if he was in his boyhood home, Dunbeath, and he told me that in certain light he could see the outline of Mormond Hill, which is in the hinterland behind my home town, Fraserburgh, from which his father's boat had on several occasions fished throughout the summer herring-fishing season. I assured him that I had seen on several occasions the Caithness Hills rise black out of the sea at sunset. I did not say then, nor would have dreamed of saying it to my boy companions, that the decent sea on which boats had just sailed over to the fishing, had me gape in astonishment as it was transformed into that unreality which Neil Gunn's words reach out to depict. The passage ends: 'And on that sea his father would be under way, or perhaps hauling in the last nets laden with the flashing silver of a great shot of herring.' So the common labour and the fabulous come together. The fishermen went to sea to catch herring to do a deal with the herring curers, of whom my father was one and who certainly dealt with Neil Gunn's father, and almost certainly hired him and his boat for a season. There was an awareness that this was no ordinary business, for the mere being at sea tended to involve the whole man, the active man and speculative man.

As early as his first novel, *The Grey Coast*, Gunn describes the characteristics common to fishermen:

Altogether a fine body of men, blue-jerseyed, easy-swaying, suntanned, with open faces, and eyes that had an unconscious trick at odd silent moments of staring past one into invisible infinitudes. And perhaps in that stare was something more than a trick. For there was gravity in it, and the longer one considered it the more that gravity seemed of the essence of their unconscious attitude to life, like a steadfastness of fine integrity.

A reason for the character of this integrity is implied:

The pulse of the sea caught them, rocked them. Ivor felt it under his feet, a gliding heave and roll, a sinuous continuous passing underneath of an insecurity that no land knew, a living insecurity taking them to itself, cutting them off with a profound sense of finality.

Gunn is interested for us, his readers, in a reality to which the sea witnesses. Its mobility, insecurity, power, above all its cosmic rhythm, is plyed in, as a composer uses a theme in tale after tale. In *The Silver Darlings* 'the slow movement of the sea became a living motion under them.' And in the same story before Finn's jump from boat to cliff there is: 'As she rose and plunged on the great impulse of the sea.' There is, of course, the direct, and thrilling description of the run in to safety in the storm in *Morning Tide* – all these are particular to seamen, but Gunn has an interest beyond the tale-telling and even the carrying of the reader into the storm. It has to do with the communication of the strange marvel of human circumstance unencumbered 'by the idea of a social duty that must keep our nose to the grindstone, the grindstone that an ever-increasing mass hysteria keeps whirling with an ever-increasing madness of momentum'. To put aside social valuations, he argues in *Off in a Boat*, is not 'escapism'. Chance puts the seaman in direct contact with that which gives him food and which destroys. He continues his argument:

 . . . one has only one life to live and that, before shuffling off, a little peace may be necessary in which to exercise one's mental attributes . . . despite all the man-made duties in the world . . . For at least nothing seems more certain finally than the loneliness of one's own self, which no mass hysteria, or political creed, or religious faith, can save from the last lonely departure that is death. It seems more than a pity to go out into that final dark without making some sort of effort to discover what glimmerings of harmony may visit the mind if we give it a reasonably receptive chance.

'Receptive' is the key word. In *The Grey Coast* Maggie and Ivor have failed to come to the understanding which both long for: 'Stiffly they stood by the byre door, looking out on the young night, but seeing nothing of the pale stars, of the dim expanse of moor, hearing no note of the sea down over the cliff-heads.' The expectation is that the young people would, unconsciously, be open to all the impressions that nature offered them, and for Ivor, the fisherman, especially the sea. In fact it is a responsiveness that sets him apart from the bookish schoolmaster who invites Ivor to come in. Here again there is a failure of a meeting of minds, but for a different reason, though the schoolmaster has an understanding of Ivor which is not communicated:

> He noted Ivor's hands, the firmness of them with the full smooth wrists above; strength, flexibility, instancy. His eyes travelled to the neck, the set of the head. Was it in the set of the head or in the expression of the face that he sensed the elusive something of self-reliance and sensitiveness, a something not of the land so much as of the sea, the uncertain sea, older than myth itself?

In this and other cases we look at people who have already been shaped by the sea.

An entry into a larger and deeper universe is frequently made in Neil Gunn's writings through the very young or very old, through those who have little experience of life, and so may not have built up resistances to new experiences, or to those old who have suffered but have not been shut in by their suffering. 'It is my belief,' wrote Edwin Muir, 'that imagination is the main faculty by which we comprehend life, however imperfectly, and are able to comprehend the people we know, including ourselves.' It is this empathetic imagination which allows the writer to identify himself or herself with people who differ from him in outlook, experience or age. For its employment there is a price to be paid in allowing the blow of experience to be felt without the sensation being guarded, but the reward is more than the understanding of another person. It may lead to a transparency of vision. The expectation of the novel, however, is the generation of interest through dialogue and social conflict. It is usually a vehicle for social comment. These interests are to be found in Neil Gunn, but his principal characters, and especially the young and the old, are drawn in the context of natural forces. Neil Gunn's final concern is in the yield of understanding that comes through those characters who are most responsive to those forces.

Gunn singled out the exactness and vividness of the descriptions of childhood in *The Guermantes Way*, the third part of Proust's *A la recherche du temps perdu*. Gunn is a modern in his consciousness of the part psychology plays in the perception of reality, and in the variable relation between the object and the subject. What the object – in Gunn's case nature, and especially natural forces – tells is dependent both on its perceiver and on its activity. Throughout the novels, and in novels, he shifts focus. One can understand the attraction of such a passage in Proust for Gunn as this:

> The bloom of the cherry tree is stuck so close to its branches, like a white sheath, that from a distance, among the other trees that shewed as yet scarcely a flower or leaf, one might have taken it, on this day of sunshine that it was still so cold, for snow, melted everywhere else, which still clung to the bushes. But the tall pear trees enveloped each house, each modest courtyard in a whiteness, more vast, more uniform, more dazzling, as if all the dwellings, all the enclosed spaces in the village were on their way to make, on one solemn date, their first communion.
>
> (Translation: C. K. Scott Moncrieff.)

What is seen by the physical eye, the fact, is immediately more than is seen. First of all Neil Gunn is a recorder. When I questioned the authenticity of some happening which seemed unlikely he said to me that I could be sure that whatever appeared nigh impossible had happened. This is the point of beginning. Because he gives the whole event, that is to say including the point of view from which it is seen, either intimately or distantly, it becomes a mental event. It seems to me as he became older he became more aware of the total experience. He may look on a deserted landscape, but he is there – a presence. Finally he may come upon himself, most probably the self as child, and 'The child is father of the man.' What he presents is in his own terms a 'positive' view. One aspect of his being positive he records in a letter to Peter Butter about Edwin Muir:

> There is a feeling of tremendous scope about him, far vistas, and sometimes one is hardly sure whether a vista backwards is in space or time, or forwards for that matter, nor does it matter much anyhow, for the experience one undergoes, if really beyond words, is yet strangely precise.
>
> But this is difficult country, though the most fascinating in the poetic realm, if one has gone far enough to glimpse an odd landscape in it. Anyway I feel quite sure that no one ever gets there until he has gone beyond his own ego.

Gunn goes on to tell Professor Butter of a meeting with Edwin Muir after the publication of Muir's collection of poems, *The Narrow Place*. Wishing to compliment the poet, he referred to a short poem which had particularly struck him:

While reading it, I saw the sea water, blue-green, sunlit, in motion, before my eyes. But may I quote it:

> The Swimmer's Death
> He lay outstretched upon the sunny wave,
> That turned and broke into Eternity.
> The light showed nothing but a glassy grave,
> Among the trackless tumuli of the sea,
> Then over his buried brow and eyes and lips
> From every side flocked in the homing ships.

Edwin told me that the poem exactly described a dream which he had had. I know we talked of the wonderful clarity and radiance of the light – of the sea – which remained in our minds from early boyhood days in that northern world. But I cannot remember if I mentioned a word in the poem which had affected me, that word 'homing'. I may have been diffident about mentioning it because I felt that such a word gave a warmth to radiance, appeared to add human experience to austere vision, and that some of his poems might gain by having it here or there, if only in the sense of gaining more readers. I know this kind of criticism is difficult if not dubious, but possibly it contains the one point I could look at here for a moment in a personal way. I don't want to repeat words like eternity, austerity, symbol, heraldic, which keep recurring in appreciations of his poetry, as if what he emotionally experienced or saw was always given a timeless shape, was translated from the fluid movements of life in the living moment into a permanence that abides where time and eternity cross. We know he had that kind of vision and could himself abide for moments in that place. But when we cannot enter into that place, into that condition of being, where what is fixed is not fixed but held in dynamic suspension, in the radiance of revelation, then we may find his poetry strangely static, lifeless, carrying life like a memory to the place beyond, where it remains forever 'frozen'. Hence the apparent lack of human warmth, so that a word like 'homing' stands out and is received somehow with gratitude.

And the light as it came after the night-fishing in *The Silver Darlings*:

> The sun rose out of the sea to find the fleet hauling their nets. The sky was high and arched and of a blue lighter than cornflowers. The clouds had been herded away to the west where a last few galleon sails were going down the horizon. The dawn spangles glittered upon the water, and the level light was reflected in the chilled faces of the fishermen, who acknowledged its thin warmth in a delicate shudder.
>
> 'It's a fine morning,' said a mouth in one boat or another, and the words were quiet as a line of poetry.

Neil Gunn said he did not recollect depicting a scene simply for the sake of a scene. Here light surrounds the fishermen and enters into them causing the simple verbal response, which 'gave a warmth to radiance'.

There is the man Neil Gunn on the way to Eigg in *Off in a Boat*:

> The wind became intermittent and the colours in the sea varied and fascinating. Towards the west, where the blue sky was widening, the water was living amaranth; east and south it was a leaden rolling waste. The cloud formations were of great complexity, from pure white puffs in the distant blue, airy as meadowland dreams, through snarls and wind-drawn angers overhead, to the sombre pall that lay on Skye and the inky gloom that blotted out the south-west.

This is the observer without any requirement to relate the vision to the tale, though the poet cannot be restrained as in 'airy as meadowland dreams'.

Then there is the small boy, Neil Gunn in *The Atom of Delight*, looking from the shore out to sea:

> On a fine summer morning the sea had a wonderful swing. Great wheels of light whirled one into another out and away. The light fell on the face, on the eyes, on the hands. It was warm and bright. It was like something new-found, and so clear that a small object here or there glittered unexpectedly like a bit of treasure . . . Off flew the

feet and, would you believe it? it was only a small stone. But look at it – queer, isn't it? See that vein. Like silver. It couldn't be silver, could it? Silver is found in stones, and gold too . . . Silver! Ho! Ho! . . . I didn't say it was silver, I said it was *like* silver . . . As the stone turned it glittered into the eye.

In Gunn's letter to Peter Butter quoted above, he went on to use the phrase 'the fluid movements of life in the living moment'. This also applies to the boy, Neil's perception of some sixty-five years previously. Substitute 'light' for life and the comment fits perfectly and relates too to a developing interest in Neil Gunn in the idea of light associated with recognition of the self. Such was this interest that he wrote an article entitled 'Light' for the summer 1968 issue of *Point*, a magazine edited by J. B. Pick in which he comments that he was struck 'by the remarkable parallelism between the birth of what we call physical life and the birth of what I have called spiritual life'. Near the end of the article he writes: 'Finally, then, an exercise in concentration, meditation and contemplation increases the chance of being struck by intuitions, intuitions on the way to a final enlightenment.'

Edwin Muir was the son of a farmer, Neil Gunn the son of a fisherman. As boy, man and poet the sea meant little to Edwin, and I think Neil Gunn was over-generous in his praise of 'The Swimmer's Death'. The word 'homing' which had a wide and deep field of reference to Gunn, had its usefulness in the poem, but to my knowledge is not used elsewhere in Muir's poetry. The land means a specific place, though Neil Gunn's landscapes frequently come near the elemental in their boulder-strewn, precipice character, but the sea has meaning at one and the same time as that which separates and that which brings together; it is local for it thunders its presence at the door, but its character is universal. Whereas each piece of landscape draws attention by its difference from any other landscape, the sea proclaims its universality. It has drama written into its constitution. Present then the word 'homing' to the seaman and the air is charged with meaning. On the one hand the activity demanded by the sea in winning its harvest precludes reflection or awareness of any other where at these times; on the other hand at other times reflection is inevitable to any thinking person.

All these aspects are reflected in the stories of Neil Gunn – the sea as actuality, as described in *Morning Tide* in the return of the boats in the storm. Hart and Pick's *A Highland Life* refers to the fictional storm in which a brother and father brought their boats to safety, and then tells how John Gunn, Neil's younger brother, was wakened by his mother, and how John

> went and stood with the harbourmaster to watch three fishing boats come straight for the small harbour in a winter gale. His brother sailed on one, his father skippered another. 'No,' John concluded, 'it's a morning that I'll never forget; and often, do you know, at moments when I've been up against it – the war and exams, and what not – that morning, with its incommunicable sense of heritage, has had its influence. It is as though one had another life, an elemental life of hidden strength, of which those bred in the towns can surely know nothing.' It happened in 1909 when John was twelve and Neil was away in Edinburgh.

Neil borrowed John's eyes for the description of the storm, and John corroborates Neil's evidence of the effect of the sea on character. Neil in *Off in a Boat* also dwelt on the effect of the sea on their heritage:

> The more I see of life the more I am convinced there is a primordial goodness in man, a natural generosity. Out of consciousness of this grows the idealism that inspires all political extremism, for it realizes, with a sort of wild and maddened anguish, how acquisitiveness and greed and colossal egoism born of power have contorted or crushed the goodness and the generosity.
>
> And of all elements for quickening the free primordial spirit of man, what can surpass the sea, with its thrill of life over the near presence of death?

This is opinion and so can be questioned. When the imagination of the artist gets to work re-creating experience, and extending it, but never putting aside its truth, we know about people, and what their environment has done to them or for them, for we become them. Neil Gunn's short story *The Telegram* begins:

I am now an old woman. The years have been going over me that fast I hardly noticed them – until this came, and now time stands in the houses and on the shore, ay, and on the little field you will be looking at from the door, hearkening.

Not 'listening' but 'hearkening', which brings you closer to the ear, but more significantly is a word belonging to a community. 'Hearken' belongs to my childhood, though not the rhythm of the old woman's speech. The words were spoken to an American soldier who, on leave, was visiting the island in the Hebrides where his 'mother's grand-father' was born: 'I raised my eyes, too, and stared over the little fields at the sea, a dark-blue sea that went flat to a remote horizon. Had the sea been really flat and my sight good enough, I could have seen the coast of my home State of Maine.' For five months the islanders had been waiting for news of a ship with men aboard who belonged to the island. Now he was in the midst of the waiting and listening, though for a short time, the island ceased to be an isolated peculiarity:

All the oceans came lapping about this remote island, and I realized that here was no primitive spot but a place that extended to the utmost corners of the earth, to all places where seamen wandered and men and women lived. My own coast of Maine and the coasts of Africa; winds over Indian and Eastern seas; empty boats and death, and the strangeness that gathers all into one old woman's voice, with the rhythm in it of the sea itself.

In this locality surrounded by the sea humanity is discovered in the few words of an old woman. Her humanity is the outcome of living in a community whose culture was shaped by their acceptance of the demands of land and sea. There was nothing between the people and these continuities. Sea and land made different demands, and demanded different attitudes to them. In *The Atom of Delight* the boy's thoughts run:

As his existence had two parents, so it had the earth and the sea. If his mother was the earth, his father was the sea. In fact he could hardly think of his father without thinking of the sea. Out of the sea came the livelihood of the household. They depended on the sea, and of all the elements in nature it was the least dependable. You could never be sure of it as you could be sure of the earth.

In Neil Gunn's novels men are the interpreters of the sea, and for the most part women of the land. The simplification does not always hold, but, through male and female, not as their being seen as symbols, but in the strengths of individual characterization, there grow beings, presences who carry the burden of human history in the setting of elemental history. We know from these people there is a right way of living through the time we are given, despite their irrelevance in terms of geological time. There is also a wrong way of living. In *The Grey Coast*:

> Jeems had to come back to the land, back to the croft, to an endless, pitiless struggling with its stony impassivity, its lean, grudging soil, its drawn-out eternity of misery, before miserliness got its claw-fingers on his soul . . . The gold was the sea's triumph.

The prising of gold means the withdrawal from the common pool of a resource. Psychologically Jeems ceases to be open to impressions from others. In this case a hard stony land has fostered aggression, a hostility to the earth itself. Earlier in *The Grey Coast* in the passage already quoted, Ivor and Maggie are out of touch with each other and also out of touch with the community out of which they have grown, the community brought together by the sharing of skills and labour, so that simple acts may give a dignity to the person. In certain circumstances they may be seen as ritual. As early as *Morning Tide* the picture has begun to be presented. Hugh has taken his father's place in the gathering of the bait and also in the landscape that in the boulders speaks of geological time, speaks at once of the land and the sea. The boy is given dignity by the other on the beach whom the boy sees first as a boulder that moves. This is the view of the person from outside seen in an elemental setting. It is a view that occurs in several of the novels that follow, in which the gesture, essential to the carrying on of the work, is held in the mind's eye. It is as if there is a momentary stopping of time. An example has been given in this essay from *The Serpent*, where Tom, the Philosopher, sees from a height 'figures singling their turnips' but I wish to take this illustration into another context. The sentence that looks forward to developments in Neil Gunn's writing is this: 'With their slightly bent heads they moved so slowly that it was easy to get the illusion of an inner meaning or design that never changed.'

In *The Telegram* the stranger/soldier has heard the reason for the islanders being held between exultation and despair, as they wait for news of the lost ship. He was 'caught now in a curious spell. It was the same kind of listening, though my mother was telling a simple story to three small children and this woman was telling the story of all humanity to a man in a soldier's uniform . . .' Only now are we in a position to 'listen', to notice the importance of small gestures against the enormous elemental background which sounds out notes of time and space. It is time for the soldier to go: 'and as I got to the crest of the slope and turned round, they waved to me, the old and the young, pausing in their harvest work to give a last farewell to the stranger.' The telegram arrives: Sheila opens it 'while the world stood still'. 'She started running out into the fields, and her high cry released all those whose feet had been held by the earth.' Yet even in this activity when another writer would have given all his attention to the scurry, there is a glance at the continuity of time: 'The old men were slower, some of them continuing to stand with the scythes in their hands, like figures of time in a story book.'

In a sense we are in 'a story book' as the 'stranger' was in one, listening to his mother as a child listens. We are put in the position of listening with the ear of innocence to, and awareness of, a tale within the tale of a universe. We are in a pause. In his letter to Peter Butter Neil Gunn comments on a view about Edwin Muir's poetry:

> as if what he emotionally experienced or saw was always given a timeless shape, was translated from the fluid movements of life in the living moment into a permanence that abides where time and eternity cross . . . But when we cannot enter into that place, into that condition of being, where what is fixed is not fixed but held in dynamic suspension, in the radiance of revelation, then we may find his poetry strangely static.

159

Gunn's characters may approach the idea of permanence in their representing continuing fundamental features of woman, man or boy, but they are subject to change, and they are presented first as individuals responding to their circumstances. Muir gives only his parents the stationary status in his *Autobiography*, but his seeing them as cut off from continuity relates to the trauma of his own experience after the family had left Orkney and suffered the misery of life and death in Glasgow. Neil Gunn's leaving his home was the outcome of his success as a scholar. Nevertheless he recognized the effects of city life as diminishing the potential of being truly alive. In his novels he stated he set out to emphasize the positive. In *The Serpent* and *The Drinking Well* the principal characters, Tom in Glasgow, and Iain in Edinburgh, return to their native country places after unsatisfactory lives in the cities in which both have had love affairs. The titles have symbolic implications and indicate a widening field of reference in the novels. The risk was the interest in concept, and in marginal experience, taking from the strength resident in the events. The requirement was that considerations of principles and theory be the outcome of the particular experience of the characters. The demand was for the writer to be open to the disruptions and cruelties which the situations of the characters provided. We witness in the greatness of Gunn's genius the acceptance of grievous harm to the beings of his people, harm done under open skies and in the presence of the earth. His most remarkable characters spring from mother earth. Out of the intensities of suffering and joy come moments where time is arrested, as when Iain, after serious illness, goes to the lambing again and is astonished by what was repeated annually:

The whole scene etched itself on his heightened mind. Such conjunctions of the seen and heard were normal enough. But as he took a step or two away, looking back, the face of the mother and the lamb came through that arrested time and place.

Here the 'arrestment', though, as Gunn put it, 'not fixed, but held in dynamic suspension', is explicit. When the impulse is strongest comprehension is unnecessary. In *The Other Landscape*, Gunn's last novel, he wrote: 'What has been unthinkable is in a moment apprehended.' Those through whom such moments are presented in

Gunn's novels are the old and young, those at the end and the beginning of life, those who present through themselves the wisdom of experience and innocence, those who know the limitations of society and through patience and suffering are capable of making a wholly human response to what has been put upon them and those responsive without reservation to the promptings of nature – the young who have neither a past nor a future, but the moment of eternity only.

Among the old one character who responds to the elements, who is of the sea and earth as none other, and who expresses in her understanding and actions all that is given her from these sources, is Dark Mairi of the Shore in *Butcher's Broom*. The book's subject matter, which deals with one of the Clearances, must have disturbed its author. On my asking why Neil had written one novel only devoted to the subject he replied, 'Because of the shame of the thing.'

'Why should you feel ashamed?' I asked him.

He replied, 'Because our own people did it.'

The comment is echoed by Tomas the Drover in *Butcher's Broom*: 'But what excuse can there be for the chiefs of our own clans, acting not in a strange land, but at home upon the hearthstones of their people.' On another occasion, the year before Neil's death, after John Gunn had shown me the burnt-out shells of cottages destroyed by the factor's men, I mentioned what I had seen to Neil. He responded, 'It's bad enough having your home burned down, it's worse having a culture destroyed.' To Francis Hart's query about the Clearances in *Butcher's Broom*, Neil replied, 'There is very little of the Clearances in *Butcher's Broom*. The tragedy is the destruction of a way of life, and the book is more about what is destroyed.'

The purifying and defining of intention had its reward in freeing the book from political and any other consideration extraneous to the focus on the effect on certain characters who bore the burden of suffering caused by the events. It left the author open to the elemental experience as he was to the cultural experience of which he knew, both from tales told and from historical studies. The factual base was important to him, for this factor concerned his integrity. Even Mairi had an origin in fact. Of course the book became a work of imagination: in this was its final truth. Houses and persons might be destroyed but the culture or an aspect of it could live on in such words as:

In the centre of this gloom was the fire, and sitting round it, their knees drawn together, their heads stooped, were the old woman, like fate, the young woman, like love, and the small boy with the swallow of life in his hand.

The lines run between fire and the flight of a bird, and so runs the book in the presence of the elements throughout, the first sentence of which telling where stands Mairi: 'The old woman stood on the Darras, the doorway, between the bright sea and the dark hills.' Seumas MacKay, an old man, is dying and Mairi talks to him: 'She took him to the sea and told him of all the people he knew or had heard of. "Yes," he whispered now and then, "yes," as if to a story of biblical remoteness.'

By taking the old man to the element from which life came, and by making it the context for hearing about 'all the people he knew or had heard of', giving the story a 'biblical remoteness', she gives dignity to his death. Her death, torn by dogs, was to be a cruel indignity. In her destruction was the destruction of a way of life. She incorporated traditions. She was the preserver and healer.

All of that sea she now carried in her basket as she went back among the companionable hills. For in addition to fish, she had many kinds of weed and shell. The clear pink dulse, gathered not off other sea-plants but off the rocks, was one of her most useful specifics. Eaten raw, it had a cleansing effect; boiled, with a pinch of butter added to the infusion, it acted as a tonic, bracing the flesh, making it supple, and drawing taut the muscles of the stomach.

She is seen on her way to her death, unknowing of its nearness:

She might have come out of the hillside; and presently she seemed to enter it again, leaving a dark boulder to mark the spot. The boulder moved and there she was coming on, small and tidy, not going anywhere so much as having business where she was at each moment, alive and wandering, like a hen or a dog.

This air of preoccupation with practical affairs was perceptible even from a long distance. The human mother carrying on her ancient solitary business with the earth, talking good and familiar sense with boulder and flower and rock, and now and then following a root below the surface; in easy accord, the communion sensible and so full of natural understanding that silence might extend into eternal silence, for wind and sun to play upon.

'The boulder moved' and she is 'now and then following a root below the surface'. In *Morning Tide* Hugh saw what appeared to be a boulder moving after he had stopped 'rooting' for tangles for his immediate pleasure and was engaged in getting mussels for bait for his father. He is thus at the beginning of an engagement to provide for the continuity of his society, although, unlike the majority of occupations today, his does not divorce him from" he processes of nature. It is through Kenn in *Highland River*, and in personal accounts of his own boyhood, that Neil Gunn celebrates the delights and understandings that come from the expression of the boy's energies in activities offered by the nature that was round him. 'From that day the river became the river of life for Kenn.' Such a celebration and enjoyment of the boy alone is possible because of the rightness of family relationships, and the functions given by life to his mother and father. He sees them thus: 'The abiding calm of his mother, old as the earth: the cleaving force of his father, like the bow of his boat.' The novelist will not let the immediacy of the elements out of the reader's mind: mother the earth, father the sea. The entire oeuvre of Neil Gunn is made in the presence of the elements. Episodes may happen in towns and cities, but the measurement of man, woman and child as persons is made in the presence of the elements, to which there is a right and wrong relationship. There is nothing forced in their pervasiveness for they are balanced by the very particular, detailed accounts of functional activities – such as the long list of salves used by Mairi in *Butcher's Broom*, of which only a part was quoted, or the detail of Kenn's hunting the salmon. The right relationships, which take account of a kind of organic whole, give meaning to life. They are stated variously but nowhere more notably than in *Highland River*.

Ultimately the shieling meant food, the river fish, and the peat-bank fire. The contacts were direct and the results were seen. There was thus about the most ordinary labour some of the excitement of creation. Nor could cold or gloom or hunger or other discomfort completely obscure the sense of family unity in its life struggle; on the contrary, as with all creative effort, the discomforts and set-backs, particularly in retrospect, add some extra quality of fineness or delight.

Gunn adds: 'Not that it worked out thus with all families by all Highland rivers.' The question for the writer is not that there occurred to the boy such complete bliss at certain moments in certain situations as to make him feel there was no other moment beyond that, that at that moment he was totally himself, but to find a means of verbal expression for it.

In *Off in a Boat* there is:

The song and the singer become oneself; then a faceless individual who sits bowed under it, nameless as a boulder in an immemorial landscape, about which the ever-shaping wind of destiny blows. Or like a rock that the sea swirls around, covering it, smothering it, to recede and come again in its undefeatable rhythm.

Here is the adult becoming one self, different from the self previous to the singing. In order to suggest the new self which is much older than the 'thinking' man, we are returned to 'an immemorial landscape' and finally to the sea with its 'undefeatable rhythm'. The second self requires an elemental association. In *The Atom of Delight*:

That the boy raced away from the social complex that normally had him in its toils, from the breeding ground of emotional ambivalence, into a freedom where with his second wind he got his second self and a powerful feeling of delight there is no doubt. This second self was his own, his very self, and he knew it, and when he stopped skipping or dancing or otherwise expressing his joy, ceased being the joy itself in its pure moment, and glanced around with a quick wary eye, he was simply making sure that nothing was going to *touch* him now.

But the boy raced from one environment to another. The 'boy's spontaneous delight' required another place: 'to apprehend the freshness, the newness, of the world, wherein an experience can be a wonder, and a memorable wonder when it pauses'. The author is alert to such moments when he is not an author, when he was off in a boat which has visited Iona and Neil Gunn's thoughts have turned to Adamnan's *Life of St Columba*: 'The most remarkable thing I discovered in Adamnan's remarkable record is this preoccupation with light as the manifestation or symbol of this goodness. The miracles are the light in legendary form.' Gunn's narrative tells a story from the 'record' to illustrate the point, and then quotes:

> St Columba, as he himself did not deny . . . in some contemplations of divine grace he beheld even the whole world as if gathered together in one ray of the sun, gazing on it as manifested before him, while his inmost soul was enlarged in a wonderful manner.

The quotation has apparently moved away from the idea of coming upon the 'second self', but Gunn in diverse situations gathers his thoughts together on 'enlightenment' or 'enlargement', or more accurately puts thought aside and so allows those understandings and intuitions which have their source in his beginnings – in loving parents, in their occupations which were rarely out of the presence of the elements, and also in the presence of his parents' beliefs, which were not Neil's. Little wonder when he looked into *Zen in the Art of Archery* by Eugen Herrigel, with its introduction by Daniel T. Suzuki, it had immediate and continuing meaning for him. In the introduction Suzuki wrote:

> Man is a thinking reed but his great works are done when he is not calculating and thinking. 'Childlikeness' has to be restored with long years of training in the art of self-forgetfulness. When this is attained, man thinks yet he does not think. He thinks like the showers coming down from the sky; he thinks like the waves rolling on the ocean; he thinks like the stars illuminating the nightly heavens; he thinks like the green foliage shooting forth in the relaxing spring breeze. Indeed, he is the showers, the ocean, the stars, the foliage.

The words apply to Neil Gunn at his best.

At the end of the film, *Light in the North*, made in 1972, Neil Gunn is seen against sea and sky. The last word he spoke as commentary was 'Miracles'.

SHORT CHRONOLOGY OF
NEIL GUNN'S LIFE AND WORKS

THE NEIL GUNN INTERNATIONAL FELLOWSHIP

FURTHER READING

INDEX TO WORKS BY NEIL GUNN

SHORT CHRONOLOGY
OF NEIL GUNN'S
LIFE AND WORKS

8 November 1891	Birth of Neil Miller Gunn in Dunbeath, a fishing village in Caithness.
1903	Moved to a married sister's home at St John's Town of Dalry, Kirkcudbrightshire. Private tutor engaged.
1907	Qualified by competitive examination for the Civil Service.
1907–9	Civil Service in London.
1909–11	Civil Service in Edinburgh.
1911	Appointed as an Excise Officer.
1921	Married Jessie Dallas Frew ('Daisy') from Dingwall.
1926	Settled in Inverness in a newly built bungalow, Larachan.
1926	*The Grey Coast* (novel).
1929	*Hidden Doors* (short stories).
1931	*Morning Tide* (novel).
1932	*The Lost Glen* (novel).
1933	*Sun Circle* (novel).
1934	*Butcher's Broom* (novel).
1937–8	*Highland River* (novel). Awarded James Tait Black Memorial Prize.

1937–8	Resigned from the Civil Service.
	Sold Larachan and bought a boat, *The Thistle*.
	Off in a Boat (a description of a voyage round the Hebrides).
	Rented Braefarm House near Dingwall in Ross & Cromarty.
1939	*Wild Geese Overhead* (novel).
	Old Music (one-act play).
	Net Results (one-act play).
1940	*Second Sight* (novel).
1941	*The Silver Darlings* (novel).
1942	*Young Art and Old Hector* (novel).
	Storm and Precipice and Other Pieces (anthology).
1943	*The Serpent* (novel).
1944	*The Green Isle of the Great Deep* (novel).
1945	*The Key of the Chest* (novel).
1946	*The Drinking Well* (novel).
1948	*The Shadow* (novel).
	The Silver Bough (novel).
	Received honorary LL.D. from Edinburgh University.
1949	*The Lost Chart* (novel).
	Highland Pack (essays).
	Moved to Kincraig, a house overlooking the Cromarty Firth on the Dingwall to Evanton Road.
1950	*The White Hour* (short stories).
1951	*The Well at the World's End* (novel).
	Moved to Kerrow House near Cannich, Inverness-shire.
	Appointed to the Crofting Commission.
1952	*Bloodhunt* (novel).
1954	*The Other Landscape* (novel).
1956	*The Atom of Delight* (autobiography).
1960	Moved to Dalcraig near North Kessock, the Black Isle.
1963	Death of his wife, 'Daisy' Gunn.

1972	Neil Gunn International Fellowship announced by Scottish Arts Council.
15 January	Death of Neil Gunn in Inverness Infirmary.
1973	Buried beside his wife in Dingwall Cemetery.

THE NEIL GUNN
INTERNATIONAL
FELLOWSHIP

THE NEIL GUNN International Fellowship, founded in 1972, shortly before Neil Gunn's death, is awarded by the Scottish Arts Council in memory of one of Scotland's greatest novelists and as a Scottish tribute to a contemporary novelist of international distinction. There is a cash award and the visiting writer is given the opportunity not only to meet writers and others involved in literature, but also to encounter other aspects of Scottish culture. Previous holders have been Heinrich Böll, Chinua Achebe, Saul Bellow, Ruth Prawar Jhabvala, Nadine Gordimer, Brian Moore, Mario Vargas Llosa and Robertson Davies.

FURTHER READING

WHAT FOLLOWS is not a bibliography of critical work on Gunn. The editors thought, however, that readers of these essays might want to know what else the writers have written about Gunn. As even that makes a rather daunting list, the items have been pruned.

All of the contributors here except Naomi Mitchison contributed to the original large-scale collection of essays edited by Alexander Scott and Douglas Gifford in 1973, *Neil M. Gunn: the Man and the Writer*, Blackwood, Edinburgh: these will not be detailed here.

Francis Russell Hart and J. B. Pick together wrote the biography, *Neil M. Gunn: A Highland Life*, Polygon, Edinburgh, 1981.

Now alphabetically:

George Bruce

'Neil Miller Gunn', an essay commissioned by the National Library of Scotland for the occasion of Neil Gunn's eightieth birthday on 8 November 1971, celebrated by an exhibition in the library.

Light in the North, a film about Neil Gunn for the occasion of his eightieth birthday, commissioned by the Scottish Film Council and the Scottish Arts Council. The scenario and interview were by George Bruce, the film produced by Pelicula.

Douglas Gifford

Neil Gunn and Lewis Grassic Gibbon, Oliver and Boyd, Edinburgh, 1983.

Dairmid Gunn

Wrote a foreword for Hart and Pick's *Neil M. Gunn: A Highland Life*, Polygon, Edinburgh, 1981.

Has also contributed forewords to reprints of eleven of Gunn's books since 1985: *The Atom of Delight, The Silver Bough, The Lost Glen, Second Sight, The Lost Chart, The Other Landscape, Off in a Boat, The Shadow, Highland Pack, The White Hour,* and *Wild Geese Overhead.*

'Authors and Houses 2: Neil M. Gunn', in *The Scottish Review* 37/8 1985, pp 38–45.

Francis Russell Hart

'The Hunter and the Circle: Neil Gunn's Fiction of Violence', *Studies in Scottish Literature*, vol I, 1963, pp 65–82.

'Beyond History and Tragedy: Neil Gunn's Early Fiction', in *Essays on Neil M. Gunn*, ed D. Morrison, Caithness Books, Caithness, 1971, pp 52–67.

'Neil Gunn', chapter 17 in *The Scottish Novel: A Critical Survey*, John Murray, London, 1978, pp 348–73.

'Neil Gunn's Drama of the Light', in *The History of Scottish Literature*, vol 4, Aberdeen University Press, Aberdeen, 1988, pp 87–102.

Naomi Mitchison

'A Self-Interview', in *Studies in Scottish Literature*, vol XIV, 1979, pp 37–51.

Gunn occasionally comes into the war diary, ed Dorothy Sheridan, *Among You Taking Notes . . .: The Waåtime Diary of Naomi Mitchison 1939–1945*, Oxford University Press, Oxford, 1985.

J. B. Pick

Neil M. Gunn: Selected Letters, Polygon, Edinburgh, 1987.

'The Work of Neil M. Gunn', *Gangrel*, no 1, 1945.

'Memories of Neil Gunn', *Studies in Scottish Literature*, vol XIV, 1979, pp 52–71.

'A Tale of Two Anti-Utopias: Orwell's *1984*, Gunn's *The Green Isle of the Great Deep*', *The Scotsman*, 17 December 1983.

Introduction to *The Atom of Delight*, 1986.

'Neil M. Gunn', in *Dictionary of National Biography* (USA), 1988.

'A Neglected Major Novel: Neil Gunn's *The Key of the Chest*', *Scottish Literary Journal*, vol 17, 1990.

INDEX TO WORKS
BY NEIL GUNN